Cockapoos

The Owners Guide from Puppy to Old Age

Choosing, Caring for, Grooming, Health, Training and Understanding Your Cockapoo Dog

By Alan Kenworthy

Copyright and Trademarks

Disclaimer and Legal Notice

Foreword

Once you've read this book, you will have all the information you need to make a well-informed decision about whether or not the Cockapoo is the breed for you, and you will know how to care for them at every stage of their life.

As an owner, expert trainer and professional dog whisperer, I would like to teach you the human side of the equation, so you can learn how to think more like your dog and eliminate behavioral problems with your pet.

While it is somewhat harder to point to predictable characteristics in a hybrid dog like a Cockapoo, this is a breed in transition. I have no doubt it will be accepted as a "stand alone" breed in years to come, which will only support the further genetic development of this exceptional pairing.

In the meantime, there are more and more responsible breeders producing excellent Cockapoos. This is not a "fad" breed, but a truly exceptional companion and one to which I look forward to introducing you.

I will try to acquaint you with all the pros and cons of life with a Cockapoo and to provide insight into canine husbandry for those people who have not lived with a dog before.

Read carefully and make your decision with a critical eye toward your time and lifestyle. I firmly believe that no adoption of any animal should be based on any primary consideration other than the welfare of the living creature that will become your sole responsibility. If you can care for a Cockapoo, I promise, the Cockapoo will care for you.

Acknowledgments

In writing this book, I also sought tips, advice, photos and opinions from many experts of the Cockapoo dog breed.

In particular I wish to thank the following wonderful experts for going out of their way to help and contribute:

USA & CANADA

Shannon Wallace of OZ Cockapoos
http://www.ozcockapoos.net/

Malinda DeVincenzi of Darby Park Doodles
http://www.darbyparkdoodles.com

Rebecca Goins of MoonShine Babies Cockapoos
http://www.moonshinebabiescpoo.com

Cristine Smith of Shady Lane Cockapoo's
http://www.shadylanekennel.net

Jackie Stafford of Dj's Cockapoo Babies
http://www.cockapoobabies.com

Jamie of Cute Cockapoos
http://www.cutecockapoos.com

Helen Downing of Family Love Kennels
http://breederofcockapoos.com/

Christy Shanklin of Christy's Cockapoos
http://www.cpuppies.com/

Acknowledgments

Phil & Adam Berthold of Homestead Cockapoos
http://www.homesteadcockapoos.com

Debbie Cowdrey of Starlo's Cockapoos
http://www.starloscockapoos.com

Jessica Sampson of Legacy Cockapoos
http://www.legacycockapoos.com/

UK

Stephen & Julia Charlton of Jukee Doodles
http://www.jukeedoodles.com

Annette Courtney of Annettes Cockapoos
http://www.annettescockapoos.co.uk/

Kirstin Pollington of Milky Paws
http://www.milkypaws.co.uk

Sylvia Hook of Sylml Cockapoo
http://www.pinetreecockapoo.co.uk

Ali Haynes of Tiddybrook Cockapoos
http://www.tiddybrookcockapoos.com

Joanna Johnson, Lincolnshire, UK
E-mail: trentdale@hotmail.com

Justine Watts of Just Dogz
http://www.justdogz.co

Table of Contents

Table of Contents

Table of Contents

Table of Contents

Table of Contents

Chapter 1 – All About the Cockapoo

The breed known today as the Cockapoo (or Cock-a-poo) was the result of chance matings of Cocker Spaniels and Poodles in the United States in the 1950s. The resulting litters were so irresistibly cute that by the 1960s, the dogs were beginning to attract attention.

Photo Credit: Stephen Charlton of Jukee Doodles

In subsequent decades, as the breed gained an international following, other variations on the name were popularized – for instance, Spoodle in Australia and Cockadoodle in Sweden. For the purposes of this discussion, however, we'll stick with "Cockapoo."

As the Cockapoo mix began to be intentionally cultivated, two types of Poodles emerged as frontrunners in the breeding pool: the Miniature and the Toy. Using these dogs, the crosses tend to be roughly the size of the Cocker Spaniel parent or just fractionally smaller. In the UK, generally the Cockapoo is 1"–2" bigger than its parents.

The Cocker Spaniel half of the equation also introduces a degree of variance because American Cocker Spaniels are slightly smaller than their English counterparts and have a longer coat. In the UK, they actively use the English Working Cocker Spaniel, the English Show Cocker Spaniel and the American Show Cocker Spaniel, all of which have distinctively different coat types.

Breed History

The practice of intentionally allowing two dogs of different breeds to produce offspring, known as crossbreeding (hybridization), is hardly new, but purists have typically frowned upon it. In recent years, however, crossbreeding has grown in popularity out of a desire to create breeds that more accurately match the changing role of dogs in our lives.

The modern pampered pooch is not the working animal of years past, nor is he a creature that lives outdoors most of his life. Dogs have firmly claimed their role as beloved family companions – in fact as members of the family – and breeders, in response, have altered their goals. Many popular crossbreed mixes are cultivated specifically for their excellent natures and for their ability to not just live, but also to thrive in a domestic setting.

Although it might be hard to imagine now, Poodles were once hunting dogs that valiantly retrieved waterfowl for their masters, willingly plunging into freezing waters to do their jobs. Modern breeders, however, look to the Poodle as the genetic source for a non-shedding coat, making the breed ideal to live cleanly indoors.

Originally, Poodles were chosen as the basis for a number of crossbreeding experiments because they were also believed to be hypoallergenic. This is not actually the case, although allergy sufferers better tolerate the dogs. We now know that the allergic reaction is caused not by cast-off hair, but by proteins in flakes of dried saliva deposited on the coat through licking.

The real aim of the original hypoallergenic crosses was to create a class of guide dogs suitable for blind people who were allergic to breeds like the iconic Labrador retriever. The result was the best known of all the "designer" dogs, the Labradoodle, whose instant popularity led to further interest in targeted crossbreeding.

The crossing of purebred Cocker Spaniels and Poodles proved equally successful due to the positive results in terms of disposition, longevity and hybrid vigor (good health.) There are far fewer cases of genetic defects in the Cockapoo than in either of its parent breeds.

This does not, however, change the fact that Cockapoos are something of a paradox, albeit a lovely one. They are indoor dogs since both sides of the pedigree are companion breeds, but they are also hunting and working dogs. You'll have an outstanding buddy in a Cockapoo, but not a lap dog!

Although either of the pedigree breeds can serve as the sire or dam in the pairing, typically the American Cocker Spaniel is the dam. English Show Cocker Spaniels and English Working Cocker Spaniels are also used, and sometimes favored, as they have even fewer genetic issues than their American cousins.

As the Cockapoo gene pool grows wider, there will be less need for out breeding, which is the practice of mating related pairs to achieve desired results. This is often done while a breed is being cultivated for official recognition, but discontinued as more acceptable mating pairs become available. Note that this is not the case in the UK, where the CCGB inbreeding co-efficient is less than 6.25% for all generations. Line breeding to homogenize the blood is not permitted.

It should be noted, however, that many Cockapoos are still "first generation" or "F1" dogs, directly resulting from the mating of a Cocker Spaniel and a Poodle. For this reason, descriptions of the dogs and of life with them still draw heavily on the perceived blending of known qualities in the pedigree foundation breeds.

Photo Credit: Phil & Adam Berthold of Homestead Cockapoos

In the United Kingdom, the Cockapoo Club of Great Britain is the official registration body for Cockapoos. They say:

"We have a strict Code of Ethics and are promoting a BREEDING standard over and above a BREED standard. We embrace the variations in appearance as this is not intended as a Show dog. As the definition of a pure breed is a dog that will breed true to type, the only way to achieve this is to in-breed to homogenize the blood, the CCGB has guidelines to keep any in-breeding co-efficient to below 6.25% – therefore it is unlikely that a common look will evolve within UK Cockapoos until we are somewhere near F9 or F10 generations. Health and fit for purpose is the primary objective and a breeder inspection protocol to ensure first hand that all CCGB Approved Breeders are ethical and truly care for their dogs and the environment that their puppies are raised. The CCGB do not vie for or indeed need or want the endorsement of any other organisation."

Physical Characteristics

Achieving a consistent look for a crossbred dog is always something of a coin toss. Cockapoos do not "breed true," meaning that it is difficult to attain predictable physical characteristics. Some Cockapoos bear a greater resemblance to their Cocker Spaniel parent, while others are more like Poodles.

All, however, are active, agile dogs. They run like the very wind, enjoy games of fetch and show an avid interest in swimming. They need regular exercise, and without it, may have a tendency to pack on the pounds. Paradoxically, however, they are perfectly happy living in small areas like apartments.

There is a great variation in color, including all of the following:

- black
- tan, in a range from beige to buff
- red, in a range from auburn to apricot
- browns (light to dark)
- sable (brown with tipping, shaded in black)
- white / cream
- silver (very rare)
- brindle (very rare)
- merle (very rare)

- roan
- phantom (black, tan and white)
- parti - black and white or brown and white

The color can be solid or the dogs can have colored patches, spots, ticking or other complex markings. The quality of the coat varies from sleek to curly, but is typically fast growing, necessitating regular grooming to prevent matting. Daily brushing is highly recommended.

Size and weight varies by the type of Poodle used in the breeding pair, with the following "standards" resulting:

- Teacup Cockapoos average less than 6 lbs. / 2.72 kg and stand under 10 inches / 25.4 cm.
- Toy Cockapoos weigh up to 12 lbs. / 5.44 kg, can reach 10 inches / 25.4 cm and tend to have a sturdy build.
- Miniature Cockapoos fall in a range of 13-18 lbs. / 5.89-6.35 kg and stand between 11-14 inches / 27.94-35.56 cm.
- Standard or Maxi Cockapoos weigh more than 19 lbs. / 8.61 kg and are at least 15 inches / 38.1 cm in stature.

Again, there can be a fairly wide degree of variation from one dog to the next, but these ranges are generally reliable. For this reason, always ask what kind of Poodle was chosen to create the Cockapoo mix. On average, the lifespan of all Cockapoos is 12 to 15 years.

In the United Kingdom, sizes differ from above. Stephen Charlton, chairman of the Cockapoo Club of Great Britain, says:

"In the UK, we have markedly different sizes for each of the categories – we don't (yet) have any Teacup Cockapoos (and nor would we want them), but we would certainly expect a UK Teacup to be well under 10 inches. Toy Cockapoos DO range from 9 inches to as much as 16 inches (we have firsthand examples in the fur here in the UK). Miniature Cockapoos on average are about 15 inches to the shoulder, though we also see them range from 10 inches through to 22 inches (genuinely factual), and Standard Cockapoos can also be between 16 and 24 inches in reality.

It's more about the genetics in the actual parents and even recessive genes that mean a breeder cannot guarantee a specific outcome unless they have older puppies for that specific pairing to compare against – we are also experiencing in the UK a greater incidence of 'sisters' being as much as an inch or two smaller than their respective 'brothers' in the majority (not all) cases."

Personality and Temperament

Understand from the beginning that Cockapoos have a reputation for being needy. They should not be left alone for long periods of time, and crate training is recommended to deal with their bouts of separation anxiety. If not addressed, this anxiety can manifest in very destructive chewing and digging, although this trait does not reflect the current reputation in the majority of English-bred Cockapoos, especially those ethically bred.

Beyond this tendency, all Cockapoo owners agree that these dogs have a unique temperament and personalities that can be a little quirky, even comical. Poodles and Cocker Spaniels are regarded as among the most intelligent of all dog breeds; so it should come as no surprise that Cockapoos are almost scary smart!

If a Cockapoo is not kept happily engaged intellectually and is allowed to become bored, you will have problems on your hands. While aggression is not at all common with these dogs, they will come up with highly inventive and usually destructive ways to keep themselves entertained. These can range from barking and jumping, to improper elimination and even self-destructive scratching.

It is imperative that a Cockapoo not be asked to just hang around all day doing nothing. Being a couch potato is not in their DNA. These dogs excel at negotiating obstacle courses and are prime candidates for agility training. They love puzzle toys and are surprisingly powerful chewers, requiring the strongest synthetic bones available. There is a positive to this fact, however, since constructive chewing relieves stress and is excellent for the animal's teeth and jaws.

You will often find the Cockapoo copying your behavior – if you are on the couch, they want to be there with you; if you are at the computer, they are laying at your feet; but if you pick up a leash – well, all of a sudden they are jumping up and down saying, "I want to go!"

So long as a Cockapoo has adequate physical and mental stimulation, you will be hard pressed to find any dog that is more consistently friendly. They are ready to play at the drop of a hat and get along brilliantly with other dogs at dog parks and daycare facilities. Often a buoyant Cockapoo takes the lead in getting quieter dogs in the middle of the current game, rather like a four-legged cruise director.

Cockapoos also have a charming reputation for their intuitive natures. They don't just pick up on your daily routines, but also on your current emotional state. This sensitivity makes them excellent therapy dogs. If you are crying, expect to have a very concerned dog at your elbow licking away your tears and trying to address and "fix" the problem.

While this is a sweet and endearing trait, in some instances it works to the detriment of the dog's wellbeing. In the presence of long-term anxiety on the part of their human, Cockapoos can dissolve into a state of nervous collapse themselves.

Certainly you can't always control what life throws at you, but realize that your dog will pick up on your state of mind and react accordingly. If you are calm, your dog will be calm.

Health

The Cockapoo is made up of a number of types of Poodles (Standard, Miniature and Toy) and Cocker Spaniels (Show Type, Working Type and American) that all come with their own health issues.

As both breeds have the potential to suffer from the same genetic eye conditions, ensure that the parents have been genetically tested for inherited conditions when purchasing a puppy or undertaking future breeding. A list of these conditions can be obtained from the Kennel Club (GB) and the American Kennel Club.

Please note that some testing and claimed test results can be a simple spot check carried out by a vet and cannot nor should not be used as an alternative to the actual genetic testing result.

Consideration is necessary when continuing the breeding of F1b, F2 and F3 puppies, along with all the necessary health checks. When breeding past F1, the buyer / breeder would need to pay extra attention to the ancestry of each parent to avoid the potential of in-breeding.

The Cockapoo Puppy

There is nothing more fun than bringing a new puppy home, even if some of that fun involves memories of epic, puppy-generated messes! Puppies are a huge responsibility no matter how much you love them, and they take a lot of work.

The first few weeks with any dog is a hugely important period of time that shapes the animal's adult behavior and temperament. What every new pet owner hopes is that in the end he will have a well-mannered, obedient and happy companion.

These goals are not just met by going through all the correct steps of puppy proofing, house training, grooming and feeding. Critical socialization must also occur, including crate training, to prevent problem behaviors like whining, biting or jumping before they become engrained habits in the dog's mind.

To achieve these goals, you have to understand the breed with which you're working. That is, frankly, not as easy with a hybrid or crossbred dog. The idea is that in combining two well-known and beloved breeds, you will get the best of both. That's a nice idea, but it doesn't always work out in practical application. It is far more difficult to predict a crossbred dog's traits. Simply put, not all Cockapoos are the same.

There are general traits that have come to be associated with the Cockapoo as the hybrid combination has become more prevalent, and these insights will continue to be refined over time. Just know from the start that you are working with a small dog equipped with a massive personality.

With Other Pets

Cockapoos are perpetually happy by disposition, affectionate and people oriented. They get along with everyone and everything: the very old, the very young and other pets.

They are, however, extremely energetic and enthusiastic dogs, qualities that may not go over well with the family cat. Both species are also known for their strong territorial urges, which can cause major clashes.

If you can't engineer a total peace agreement, détente is usually an option. Do not force the animals to interact or to spend time together. When the puppy first arrives, put the little dog in its crate and allow the cat to check out the new arrival. Expect feline caution and disapproval, often vocal.

Supervise all subsequent interactions, reinforcing good behavior with treats and praise, but not over-reacting to aggression or "trash talking." At this stage, the puppy is likely the one in need of rescuing from potential sharp-clawed swipes. Just separate the animals with a firm "no" and try again later. Understand that this can go on for several weeks until your pets reach some form of agreement whose terms only they will fully understand.

As for other kinds of pets, exercise reasonable caution and use your common sense. Obviously no dog should be allowed to play with a rabbit, for instance. By and large, however, Cockapoos leave other animals alone. The reason they're so bad to devil the family cat is because they'll get a reaction. A gold fish floating in a bowl or a bird sitting in a cage is not nearly so interesting.

With Children

Cockapoos have an excellent reputation for getting along well with children so long as the children have been taught how to properly and kindly interact with them (or with any animal.) Regardless, you should not leave a young child unsupervised with a dog. If a child hurts the dog by pulling its ears or tail or even biting the creature, the dog can hardly be blamed for reacting.

That being said, Cockapoos are truly gentle dogs. Because of their strongly empathetic natures, they will tend to put up with a great deal from children that other dogs would not. For this reason, it's generally the welfare of the dog rather than that of the child that is a matter of concern.

If a Cockapoo were to be aggressive, we can probably blame unethical breeders using any available parent dog to breed from, purely for profit, without any care for a selection criteria that would render them fit for the purpose of breeding a family pet.

Male or Female?

In my opinion, the only time that gender is a major consideration is if you are intending to breed the dog, otherwise, you should be more focused on the individual Cockapoo's personality. In most instances, however, people want female puppies because they assume they will be sweeter and gentler.

There is no valid basis for this assumption, however, and it should not be the major reason for rejecting a male dog out of hand. Either gender can be dominant, aggressive, stubborn or territorial. The real determining factor in any dog's long-term behavior is the quality of its training in relation to its place in the family. Consistency in addressing bad behaviors before they start is crucial.

Many breeders agree that adult female dogs that have been unduly coddled as puppies tend to display more negative behavior and greater territoriality than males. This is a factor to consider if you are in the position of adopting a fully-grown Cockapoo, especially in a rescue situation.

The greatest negative behaviors cited for male dogs are spraying and territorial urine marking. In the case of purebred adoptions, having the animal spayed or neutered is typically a condition of the purchase agreement. Kennels most often make pet-quality animals available because they do not conform to the accepted breed standard sufficiently to participate in a breeding program or to be shown. Spaying and neutering under these circumstances protects the integrity of the kennel's bloodlines.

Since Cockapoos are not purebred dogs, this provision may or may not be part of a formal adoption agreement. Regardless, it is highly advisable to have the animal "altered" before 6 months of age. The reduction in hormone levels stops problem behaviors, like spraying in males or moodiness when a female is in heat, and also lessens tendencies toward territorial aggression.

Puppy or Adult Dog?

People are drawn to puppies for all the obvious reasons. They are adorable, and the younger the dog is at adoption, the longer you will have with your pet. At an average of 12 to 15 years, Cockapoos are relatively long lived for their size. If you do find an adult dog in need of adoption, longevity will most likely not be a "deal breaker" in your decision to welcome the animal into your home.

I am a huge advocate of all animal rescue organizations. The numbers of homeless companion animals in need of adoption stands at shocking levels. To give one of these creatures a "forever" home is an enormous act of kindness. You will literally be saving a life.

Cockapoos are wonderful dogs, and if you have your heart set on one, I fully understand why. But if you are simply searching for a loyal four-legged friend of any breed, please do not rule out a shelter adoption.

Even if you do decide to go the route of adopting a hybrid or designer dog, please support the work of rescue organizations with your donations and volunteer hours. These groups are chronically in need of help.

When you do adopt a rescue dog, find out as much as possible about the dog's background and the reason why it was given up for adoption. With Cockapoos, you will rarely find that one has been surrendered for being aggressive in any way. In most cases, the dogs have simply proved to be too much for the previous owners, who did not understand the breed's issue with separation anxiety and need for exercise and mental stimulation.

Many pets are surrendered when an elderly owner becomes too sick to care for the animal or passes away. This is a common story with Cockapoos found in rescue situations because the breed is so very good with the elderly.

One or Two?

When you're sitting down in the middle of the floor surrounded by frolicking Cockapoo puppies, your heart may tell you to go ahead and get two, but it's generally best to take a deep breath and listen to your brain. Just owning one dog is a serious commitment of time and money.

If you do get the second dog, *everything* doubles: food, housebreaking lessons, training sessions, vet bills, boarding fees and *time*. You may well reason that two dogs will keep each other company, and that is true up to a point, but Cockapoos need their humans. Instead of having just one adorable canine lord and master, you're setting yourself up to answer to two.

The good thing about Cockapoos is that they are friendly and adaptable. If you do decide you want a second dog, adding to the family later won't be a problem. I would suggest pacing yourself. Start with one dog and put off a second adoption for the future.

The Need for Socialization

Any breed, no matter how well regarded in terms of temperament, can still develop bad habits to the point of being obnoxious. Puppies should begin training as soon as possible, preferably at 10-12 weeks of age.

Regarding the exposure of puppies to other dogs, I recommend that a puppy is not placed on the ground in any public place until it is fully vaccinated. However, socialization and exposure to the outside world is invaluable to a puppy's development in the early stages — say, the first 8 to 16 weeks.

Carry a puppy to a safe place: a veterinary practice's puppy party or a friend or family's enclosed garden, where only fully vaccinated dogs are or have been present (ensuring that space is free from foxes and fox waste), as interaction with other dogs, people and places will aid their development and adjustment into the complex role that they will have to live in, that is living with a human family.

Also, understand that you will be in "school" as much as your Cockapoo. Dogs will quite happily get away with murder if they get their paws on a compliant human. It is your job to be the "leader of the pack," a responsibility for which many humans are ill equipped without some in-class time of their own!

Famous Cockapoos and Their Owners

As an illustration of just how popular Cockapoos have become, these beguiling dogs have found their way into the hearts of some pretty famous folks. Actress and political activist Ashley Judd is among the most recognized and vocal supporters of this designer breed, working with a charitable group called Cockapoo Crazy. She has taken her own Cockapoos, Shug and Buttermilk, on to red carpets and film sets, greatly enhancing the visibility of the breed.

Billie Joe Armstrong, from the group Green Day, owns a Cockapoo named Rocky who has joined the singer for a highly popular YouTube vocal video. Lady Gaga named her Cockapoo Fozzi and accompanies her everywhere.

Sammi "Sweetheart" Giancola of the reality TV show "Jersey Shore" adopted a Cockapoo named Kylie in 2011, while Jensen Ackles of the series "Supernatural" and his wife Daneel Harris Ackles have shared their home with Icarus since 2007. He's a frequent traveler, going back and forth with his humans between Vancouver and Los Angeles.

Other celebrities who share their lives with devoted Cockapoo pals include Lena Dunham, Minka Kelly, Julie Anne Rhodes, Maria Shriver, Lindsay Ellington, Mary Anne Rajskub and best-selling author Lynda La Plante.

Chapter 2 - Cockapoo Dog Breed Standard

Understanding that the Cockapoo is a designer dog and is not yet recognized by any official governing body within the dog fancy, the following breed standard (which I am reproducing verbatim with only paragraph breaks inserted for readability) is used by the American Cockapoo Club. It will give you an idea of what breeders who are actively working to standardize the breed currently consider the ideal qualities for a Cockapoo.

Photo Credit: Sylvia Hook of Sylml Cockapoo

General Appearance

Cockapoos have a sturdy, squarely-built appearance. The length from the body measured from the breastbone to the rump is approximately the same to slightly longer than the height from the highest point of the shoulder to the ground.

He stands up well at the shoulder on straight forelegs with a top line that is level to slightly sloping toward moderately bent hindquarters. He is a dog capable of great speed and endurance, combined with agility.

The body must be of sufficient length to permit a straight and free stride. Cockapoos should never appear low and long, or tall and gangly, but should always be in proportion.

Size and Weight

Size of Cockapoos can be influenced by either parent's recent background. Adult dogs 10" at the shoulder or less are toy size. Dogs 11"-14" at the shoulder are considered mini size, and those 15" at the shoulder and over are standard size. Cockapoo size is judged by their height, not their weight. Two dogs who are the same size can vary considerably in weight depending both on their overall build and whether one is fat or thin. Weights of individuals will depend on the factors explained above. To give a general idea of weight, a toy would ideally weigh under 12 pounds, a mini 13-20 pounds and a standard 21 pounds and up.

Head

Expression. Large, round, well-set, well-spaced eyes with a keen, soulful, endearing and intelligent expression. The color of the eyes should be dark brown on dogs with black noses. Brown dogs have brown noses. Dogs with light-colored noses may have lighter (i.e.: greenish, hazel) eyes. The eyes should not have a droopy appearance.

Hair should be scissored back so as not to obstruct the eyes or vision. The ears should hang fairly close to the head, starting above the eyes and hanging to well below eye level. They should be well-feathered, but never erect or carried up over the head. Ideally the bottom of the ears should be level with the beard. The skull is moderately rounded but not exaggerated, with no tendency towards flatness.

Bite

Aligned bite, with neither over- nor under-bite. Level bites (incisors striking edge to edge) are acceptable, but scissors bite (lower incisors striking just behind the uppers) is preferred.

Neck, Top Line, Body

The neck rises strongly from the shoulders and arches slightly as it tapers to join the head. Carried high and with dignity, the neck is never pendulous (no throatiness – skin tight). The top line is level to slightly sloping toward the hindquarters. The chest is deep and moderately wide, with well-sprung ribs, its lowest point no higher than the elbow.

Tail

The tail is set on line with the back and carried on line with the top line or higher; when the dog is in motion the tail action is merry. The tail can be left long or docked like the parent breeds; both are acceptable. The tail should be well feathered and full coated when left long. If not docked, the tail is to be curled up over the back and left long, never shaven. If docked, tail should be no more and no less than 4 inches.

Forequarters

The shoulders are well laid back, forming an angle with the upper arm of approximately 90 degrees, permitting easy movement and forward reach. When viewed from the side with the forelegs vertical, the elbow is directly below the highest point of the shoulder blade.

Forelegs are parallel, straight, with strong pasterns. Legs should be set close to the body. Front dew claws can be left or removed, back dew claws should be removed. Feet should be in balanced proportion with the dog; however, the feet should be compact, with arched toes and turn neither in nor out.

Hindquarters

When viewed from behind, the legs are parallel when in motion and at rest. Moderately angled at the stifle, and clearly defined thighs. When standing, the rear toes should be behind the point of the rump.

Coat Types

As with many other breeds, Cockapoos have three different coat types. There is the tight curly coat, the medium curl, and the flat coat. While we strive for the medium curl, all three coat types are acceptable. It is very common to see all three types within the same litter of pups. This can happen with 1st, 2nd, 3rd (etc.) generation litters.

Coat Length

The Cockapoo's coat should be clipped all over in a "teddy bear" type cut of about 2-3". The top of the head should be the same length as the body. If the tail is docked, the hair on the docked tail should be the same length as the body.

A Cockapoo should never be shaven. They should have facial hair and a beard, all flowing into each other and trimmed no longer than 4 inches. The ears should be trimmed straight across and even with the bottom of the beard.

The face should never be shaven. If the dog is not being shown, then a shorter or longer coat is allowed. Just remember to keep the eyes clear of fur and keep them well brushed.

Color and Markings

Any solid color; parti color (two or more solid colors, one of which must be white); phantom (brown, black or silver body with contrasting color on legs, under tail, eyebrows, side of face, inside ears); sable (may be black, brown, brindle, changing to silver, silver/gold mix, red, brown, other, all with darker points); tri-color (parti color with white base and tan markings over each eye, on the sides of the muzzle/cheeks, on the underside of the ears, on all feet and/or legs and optionally on the chest). Merle and/or roan are also acceptable colors. The nose and rims of eyes should be one solid color. Brown-colored dogs may have brown noses, eye rims, lips, dark toenails and dark amber eyes. Black, blue, gray, cream and white dogs have black noses, eye rims and lips, black or self-colored toenails and very dark eyes. In light-colored dogs, the liver-colored nose is quite common.

Temperament

Cockapoos are very people-oriented, outgoing and happy dogs. The playful personality appeals to young and old alike. The Cockapoo has a keen intelligence any adult can appreciate, coupled with a forgiving nature that makes it unparalleled as a children's dog. They are as much at home in an apartment as they are on the biggest farm. They are extremely easy to train in just about any situation, but are people dogs and should not be left alone for extended periods of time.

(*Source*: http://www.americancockapooclub.com/)

Note that this entire section is only applicable to American Cockapoos. The Cockapoo Club of GB (CCGB) actively rejects the need or notion of putting a "Standard" look over and above the health and nature of this family pet dog.

Chapter 3 – Getting Serious About Owning a Cockapoo

When you have moved past the stage of just "window shopping" for a dog and think you're pretty well settled on a Cockapoo, there are questions you need to ask yourself and some basic education you should have before you progress to actually getting a dog.

Is a Cockapoo the Dog for You?

With a pedigreed dog, it's often easier to determine if a breed is or isn't a good fit in a given situation. My late father was, in his own way, a dog whisperer and for the bulk of his life had nothing but "mutts," which is just a colloquialism for a crossbred dog.

It was not until his health began to fail that he became interested in Yorkshire Terriers because they exhibited the qualities of loyalty and feistiness he valued, but in a small, manageable "package."

Cockapoos are not, however, the product of random hybridization. They are, under the best of circumstances, a workable combination of qualities present in two well-documented breeds.

Under poor circumstances, they are the product of careless breeding and thus a bit of a genetic mess, a problem that can be sidestepped by careful acquisition from reputable sources.

The kinds of questions you want to ask yourself must, in so far as it is possible to do so, bridge all the potential ups and downs of owning a designer dog:

- Can your life accommodate the physical and emotional needs of a small, but highly energetic breed with known issues regarding intellectual stimulation and separation anxiety?

- Will you commit to brushing your dog daily and to having the animal professionally groomed every 4-6 weeks to keep its fast-growing coat in good condition and free of mats?

- Due to the breed's fondness for water, do you understand the need for your pet's ears to be kept clean and dry? If moisture is allowed to remain trapped in the ear canal, the resulting bacterial and fungal infections can cost the Cockapoo its hearing. Potential ear problems are the breed's inheritance from the Cocker Spaniel side of their lineage.

- Are you okay with the fact that even though you may

have a "look" in mind, all crossbred puppies will be different in terms of their size, color, coat, temperament, level of activity and general health?

- You will not have the same level of consistency in choice that is the hallmark of purebred dogs purchased from kennels with carefully crafted bloodlines.

The primary choices with which you will be confronted when you do begin to seriously look for a dog are "male or female" and "puppy or adult." While some people feel this simplifies the matter greatly, there are specific considerations relative to both of these choices.

Finding and Picking a Puppy

Typically, the first step in finding a specific type of puppy is tracking down a breeder. Thankfully in the case of the Cockapoo, the hybrid mix is becoming sufficiently well established, especially in the United States and Great Britain, that there are good resources for locating dogs.

The American Cockapoo Club:
http://www.americancockapooclub.com

The Cockapoo Club of Great Britain:
http://www.cockapooclubgb.co.uk

Learn Basic Health Evaluation Tips

Before the "Aw Factor" kicks in and you are completely swept away by the cuteness of a Cockapoo puppy, familiarize yourself with the basic quick health checks you should make as you are playing with a young dog up for adoption.

- Although a puppy may be sleepy at first, the dog should wake up quickly and be both alert and energetic.

- The little dog should feel well fed in your hands, with some fat over the rib area.

- The coat should be shiny and healthy with no dandruff, bald patches or greasiness.

- The puppy should walk and run easily and energetically with no physical difficulty or impairment.

- The eyes should be bright and clear with no sign of discharge or crustiness.

- Breathing should be quiet, with no excessive sneezing or coughing and no discharge or crust on the nostrils.

- Examine the area around the genitals to ensure there is no visible fecal collection or accumulation of pus.

- Test the dog's hearing by clapping your hands when it is looking away from you and judging the puppy's reaction.

- Test the vision by rolling a ball toward the dog, making sure the puppy appropriately notices and interacts with the object.

Locating Breeders to Consider

When you have educated yourself about what to look for in a healthy puppy, move on to visiting breeder websites or speaking over the phone to breeders in whose dogs you are interested. You want to arrive at a short list of potential kennels. Plan on visiting more than one before you make your decision.

If you do not have a national Cockapoo organization or club in your country, you will be faced with searching for breeder sites online. I will discuss evaluating breeders more fully in the chapter on buying a Cockapoo.

For now, know that your best option is to obtain a dog from a kennel that is clearly serious about its breeding program and displays this fact with copious information about their dogs, including lots and lots of pictures.

Photo Credit: Kirstin Pollington of Milky Paws

Finding advertisements for Cockapoos in local newspapers or similar publications is dicey at best. You may simply be dealing with a "backyard breeder," a well-meaning person who has allowed the mating of two dogs of different pedigrees. There is nothing inherently wrong with this situation, although I do strongly recommend that an independent veterinarian evaluate the puppy before you agree to adopt it.

All too often, however, if you go through the classified ads you can stumble into a puppy mill where dogs are being raised in deplorable conditions for profit only.

Never adopt any dog unless you can meet the parents and siblings and see for yourself the surroundings in which the dog was born and is being raised. If you are faced with having to travel to pick up your dog, it's a huge advantage to see recorded video footage, or to do a live videoconference with the kennel owner and the puppies.

It is far, far preferable to work with a kennel where you can verify the health of the parents and discuss with a knowledgeable breeder the potential for any congenital illnesses.

Responsible breeders are more than willing to give you all this information and more, and are actively interested in making sure their dogs go to good homes. If you don't get this "vibe" from someone seeking to sell you a dog, something is wrong.

The Timing of Your Adoption Matters

Be highly suspicious of any kennel that assures you they have dogs available at all times. It is normal, and a sign that you are working with a reputable kennel, when your name is placed on a waiting list.

(You may also be asked to place a small deposit to guarantee that you can adopt a puppy from a coming litter. Should you choose not to take one of the dogs, this money is generally refunded, but find out the terms of such a transaction in advance.)

Typically females can only conceive twice a year, so spring or early summer is generally the best time to find a puppy. Breeders like to schedule litters for the warm months so they can train their young dogs outside.

Think about what's going on in your own life. Don't adopt a dog at a time when you have a huge commitment at work or there's a lot of disruption around an impending holiday. Dogs, especially very smart ones like Cockapoos, thrive on routine. You want adequate time to bond with your new pet, and to help the little dog understand how his new world "runs."

Also, remember that Cockapoos are highly people-oriented dogs and easily suffer from separation anxiety. You don't want to be rushed in the beginning of this new relationship.

Approximate Purchase Price

Targeting a price for an emerging breed like the Cockapoo can be difficult. You may well see newspaper listings for puppies as low as $200 / £120, but you have no way of guaranteeing the health of a dog bred in "backyard" circumstances.

To be 100% certain you are getting the best quality dog whose genetics have been fully considered, expect to pay $750-$1900 / £200-£1200 (in the UK) depending on location and kennel.

Rescue Organizations and Shelters

When you are considering rescuing a specific breed of dog or puppy, the first place to start your search will be with your local shelter and rescue groups, as well as local breeders.

You can expect to pay an adoption fee to cover the cost of spaying or neutering, which will be only a small percentage of what you would pay a breeder and will help to support the shelter or rescue facility by defraying their costs.

The Cockapoo Club of Great Britain runs an active and effective non-profit making RRR section supported by The Dogs Trust in the UK. Re-homing should not be seen as a cheap way to get a Cockapoo; although variable in amount, a goodwill donation is customary when adopting a Cockapoo. The ongoing costs, care, attention and suitability of keeping a dog are identical whether the dog is bought from a breeder as a puppy or if indeed it is rescued.

Pros and Cons of Owning a Cockapoo Dog

Talking about pros and cons for any breed always draws me up a little short. It's a very subjective business since what one person may love in a breed another person will not like at all.

I think Jack Russell Terriers are fantastically smart dogs, but they are also the drill sergeants of the canine world. I don't have any desire to give my life over to a dog that will run it at that level. My preference is for more laid-back breeds that value a good nap as highly as a rousing game of fetch.

People who love Cockapoos should be as ready to talk about their good qualities as well as the challenges they pose for one overriding reason – a desire to see these very special animals go to the best home possible where they will be loved and appreciated.

Reasons to Adopt a Cockapoo Dog

- Cockapoos are great family pets, exhibiting affection and loyalty, but also with a truly fun-loving spirit. They get along equally well with the very young and the very old.

- Although active dogs with a need for daily exercise and intellectual stimulation, they still live quite happily in small spaces like apartments.

- The Cockapoo breed is so empathetic and sensitive to emotions that they are often used as therapy animals.

- Cockapoos typically interact well with other pets, but can be a trial and tribulation to the family cat until the animals work out the terms of their own peace agreement.

- Cockapoos are highly intelligent and learn quickly.

Reasons NOT to adopt a Cockapoo Dog

- Cockapoos are highly people oriented and suffer from separation anxiety if they are left alone for long periods of time. This can lead to problem behaviors, including barking, scratching, digging and chewing, among others, although in fairness to Cockapoos, any dog can develop separation anxiety if not trained and socialized appropriately.

- Although Cockapoos don't shed much, their hair does grow very quickly. They will need to be groomed every 4-6 weeks and brushed several times a week to keep mats from forming.

- Because these dogs are so intelligent and need adequate mental stimulation, they easily suffer from boredom that can be displayed in destructive behaviors like digging, chewing and barking.

- If not well trained, a Cockapoo's native exuberance can be expressed in inappropriate jumping accompanied by demanding and insistent whining.

- Because Cockapoos are a hybrid or "designer" breed, it is more difficult to find an individual that conforms to a specific "look" you may have in mind.

Chapter 4 – Buying a Cockapoo

Purchasing a pedigreed dog or a designer dog like a Cockapoo is not always the kind of casual adoption process with which most people are familiar.

Photo Credit: Stephen Charlton of Jukee Doodles

If you are adopting a pedigreed animal, you are immediately confronted with the question of pet versus show quality. With pet-quality adoptions, you will almost certainly be required to spay or neuter the dog before it reaches six months of age in order to take possession of the registration papers.

When adopting a crossbred dog, however, you may be looking at almost any kind of "deal" absent or inclusive of the typical health guarantees, genetic information, medical records and other details of a pedigree adoption arrangement.

How to Choose a Breeder

Personally, I am not an advocate of shipping live animals. Try find a local breeder, or one in reasonable traveling distance from your home. Even if your primary means of searching out a Cockapoo breeder is the Internet, you should visit the breeder at least once before adopting the dog and plan on picking the animal up in person.

Be extremely suspicious of any breeder who is not willing to allow such a visit or seems reticent about showing you the kennel once you are on site. You don't want to interact with just one puppy. You should be allowed to meet the parent(s) and the entire litter.

It's important to get a sense of how the dogs live and the level of care they receive. In your discussions with the breeder, you should have the feeling that information is flowing freely in both directions and that the individual is being forthcoming about both the positives and negatives of the Cockapoo cross.

What to Expect From a Good Breeder

Responsible breeders help with the process of selecting a puppy and place the long-term welfare of the dog at the center of the discussion. The breeder should be interested in your life, asking questions about your schedule, family and other pets. This is not a sign of someone being nosy, but rather an indication of an expert judging the correctness of the placement. Breeders who don't seem interested in what kind of home the dog will have may very well not be on the up and up.

Ideally the Breeder Should Provide the Following

Again, because Cockapoos are not an officially sanctioned breed, you may be dealing with a less formal adoption process. However, in the best of all possible worlds, the breeder will treat the arrangements as if the dog you are adopting is pedigreed, and will provide the following items to you:

- *contract of sale* – This document should detail the responsibilities of both parties in the adoption and explain how any paperwork or records will be transferred to you.

- *information packet* – This material should include advice on feeding, training and exercise, as well as necessary health procedures like worming and vaccinations.

- *description of ancestry* – The breeder should include some description of the dog's ancestry, including the names and specific types of Cocker Spaniel and Poodle used to create the mix.

- *existing health records* – You should have a record of all medical procedures the dog has required, as well as a record of vaccinations received and a schedule for booster shots. If there is any concern about potential genetic issues, that information should also be fully disclosed in writing.

- *health guarantee* – At the very least, you should receive a guarantee of the puppy's health at the time of adoption. In pedigreed adoptions, purchasers are asked to confirm this fact with a vet within a set period of time. Although you may not be required by the terms of the purchase to have such an immediate health evaluation, it's a very good idea to do so.

- Sample of food to start feeding new puppy.

- Scented blanket of mum and other litter mates.

Warning Signs of a Bad Breeder

Always be alert to key warning signs like:

- Breeders who tell you it is not necessary for you to visit the kennel in person.

- Assertions that you can buy a puppy sight unseen with confidence.

- Breeders who will allow you to come to their home or kennel but will not show you where the dogs live.

- Homes or kennels where dogs are kept in overcrowded conditions and as a consequence seem nervous and apprehensive.

- Situations in which you are not allowed to meet at least one of the puppies' parents.

- Sellers who are unable to produce health information for the parents and the puppies, or claims that the records will be produced at a later date.

- No health guarantee provided and no discussion of what happens if the puppy does fall ill, including the potential for a refund of the purchase price.

- Refusal to provide a signed bill of sale or vague assurances that one will be forwarded to you later.

Avoiding Scam Puppy Sales

No one wants to support a puppy mill, even unwittingly. Such operations exist for profit only. They crank out the greatest number of litters possible with an eye toward nothing but the bottom line. The care the dogs receive ranges from deplorable to non-existent. Inbreeding is standard, leading to genetic abnormalities and wide-ranging health problems.

The Internet is, unfortunately, a ripe advertising ground for puppy mills, as are pet shops. It is a sad corollary to the growing popularity of "designer dogs" that puppy mills are seeing a profit base in these combinations and engaging in unscrupulous breeding practices.

Some scammers will advertise a single puppy on the free-to-advertise websites and get you to pay a "deposit" over the Internet. They leave the advert open long enough to rake in a number of deposits then remove the ad and create a new one from a different location.

Many breeders are not what they appear to be. They often have multiple websites, phone numbers and email addresses for each breed they sell. All of their dogs may not be at the same location or they work together with friends or family to help hide these facts. A good website is easy to create. Do some snooping around using Google, online white pages, GIS, tax, maps etc. and you might be surprised at what you find out.

Again, if you cannot visit the kennel where the puppies were born, meet the parents, inspect the facilities and receive some genetic and health information on the dog *something is wrong*.

Best Age to Purchase a Puppy

A Cockapoo puppy needs time to learn important life skills from the mother dog, including eating solid food and grooming themselves.

For the first month of a puppy's life, they will be on a mother's milk-only diet. Once the puppy's teeth begin to appear, they will start to be weaned from mother's milk, and by the age of 8 weeks should be completely weaned and eating just puppy food.

Puppies generally leave between 7-9 weeks and are usually weaned before they receive their first vaccines. It is not beneficial for the pup to stay longer, as it can have a negative affect for several reasons. One is that the puppy should not have access to nursing after their first vaccine, otherwise that vaccine is void. Some moms will continue to nurse despite the puppy being on solid food.

In other cases, the mom is too overwhelmed with the size of the pups and the size of the litter and she avoids them. This occurs as early as 6 weeks old and can result in bad behaviors as the puppies interact with each other. Their roughhouse playing becomes more and more imprinted on them, and families could struggle to teach the puppy not to play with children as they do with their litter mates.

Trainers would even highly recommend training and bonding begin with their new families by 8-10 weeks. In addition, pups need to be highly socialized between 8-12 weeks with new people, new experiences and places. This time period is very crucial in developing a well-rounded pup.

With vet approval being required in some states, a breeder can place pups a little earlier than 8 weeks if the puppies show signs of being properly weaned and being socially mature enough. In fact, every mommy/litter experience will be a little different. It's up to the breeder to evaluate each litter individually and determine the best timing for release based primarily on proper weaning and maturity.

How to Pick a Puppy?

My best advice is to go with the puppy that is drawn to you. My standard strategy in selecting a pup has always been to sit a little apart from a litter and let one of the dogs come to me. My late father was, in his own way, a "dog whisperer." He taught me this trick for picking puppies and it's never let me down.

I've had dogs in my life since childhood and enjoyed a special connection with them all. I will say that often the dog that comes to me isn't the one I might have chosen — but I still consistently rely on this method.

Photo Credit: Annette Courtney of Annettes Cockapoos

Beyond that, I suggest that you interact with your dog with a clear understanding that each one is an individual with unique traits. It is not so much a matter of learning about all Cockapoos, but rather of learning about YOUR Cockapoo dog.

You will want to choose a puppy with a friendly, easy-going temperament, and your breeder should be able to help you with your selection. Also ask the breeder about the temperament and personalities of the puppy's parents and if they have socialized the puppies.

Always be certain to ask if a Cockapoo puppy you are interested in has displayed any signs of aggression or fear, because if this is happening at such an early age, you may experience behavioral troubles as the puppy becomes older.

Check Puppy Social Skills

When choosing a puppy out of a litter, look for one that is friendly and outgoing, rather than one who is overly aggressive or fearful. Puppies who demonstrate good social skills with their litter mates are much more likely to develop into easy-going, happy adult dogs that play well with others.

Observe all the puppies together and take notice:

Which puppies are comfortable both on top and on the bottom when play fighting and wrestling with their litter mates, and which puppies seem to only like being on top?

Which puppies try to keep the toys away from the other puppies, and which puppies share?

Which puppies seem to like the company of their litter mates, and which ones seem to be loners?

Puppies that ease up or stop rough play when another puppy yelps or cries are more likely to respond appropriately when they play too roughly as adults.

Is the puppy sociable with humans? If they will not come to you, or display fear toward strangers, this could develop into a problem later in their life.

Is the puppy relaxed about being handled? If they are not, they may become difficult with adults and children during daily interactions, grooming or visits to the veterinarian's office.

Check Puppy's Health

Ask to see veterinarian reports to satisfy yourself that the puppy is as healthy as possible. Before making your final pick of the litter, check for general signs of good health, including the following:

1.   Breathing: will be quiet, without coughing or sneezing, and there will be no crusting or discharge around their nostrils.
2.   Body: will look round and well fed, with an obvious layer of fat over their rib cage.
3.   Coat: will be soft with no dandruff or bald spots.
4.   Energy: a well-rested puppy should be alert and energetic.
5.   Hearing: a puppy should react if you clap your hands behind their head.
6.   Genitals: no discharge visible in or around their genital or anal region.
7.   Mobility: they will walk and run normally without wobbling, limping or seeming to be stiff or sore.
8.   Vision: bright, clear eyes with no crust or discharge.

Chapter 5 – Caring for Your New Puppy

All puppies are veritable forces of nature, but this is doubly true for an active, curious and engaged Cockapoo. They are little dogs that can get in big trouble before you even know what's happened. The first job ahead of you – and I do mean *before* you bring your new pet home – is to puppy proof the house!

Photo Credit: Stephen Charlton of Jukee Doodles

The Fundamentals of Puppy Proofing

Think of a puppy as a very bright toddler with four legs. Get yourself in the mindset that you're bringing a baby genius home, and try to think like a puppy. Every nook and cranny is a challenge, a curiosity waiting to be explored. That inquisitive nose will go into all of them, and every discovery is in danger of being chewed, swallowed – or both!

Take a complete inventory of the areas to which the dog will be given access, and remove all lurking poisonous dangers from cabinets and shelves. Get everything up and out of the dog's reach. Pay special attention to cleaning products, insecticides, mothballs, fertilizers and antifreeze.

Look Through Your Puppy's Eyes

Get down on the floor and have a look around from puppy level. Anything that catches your attention will surely be spotted by your new furry Einstein.

Do not leave any dangling electrical cords, drapery pulls or even loose scraps of wallpaper. Look for forgotten items that have gotten wedged behind cushions or kicked under the furniture. Don't let anything stay out that is a potential choking hazard.

Tie up anything that could be a "topple" danger. A coaxial cable may look boring to you, but in the mouth of a determined little dog, it could bring a heavy television set crashing down. Cord minders and electrical ties are your friends!

Remove stuffed items and pillows, and cover the legs of prized pieces of furniture against chewing. Take anything out of the room that even looks like it *might* be a toy. Think I'm kidding? Go online and do a Google image search for "dog chewed cell phone" and shudder at what you will see.

Plant Dangers, Inside and Out

The list of indoor and outdoor plants that are a toxic risk to dogs is very long and includes many surprises. You may know that apricot and peach pits are poisonous to canines, but what about spinach and tomato vines?

The American Society for the Prevention of Cruelty to Animals has created a large reference list of plants for dog owners here.

http://www.aspca.org/pet-care/animal-poison-control/toxic-and-non-toxic-plants

Go through the list and remove any plants from your home that might make your puppy sick. Don't think for a minute that your dog will leave such items alone. He won't!

Preparing for the Homecoming

Before you bring your new puppy home, purchase an appropriate travel crate and a wire crate for home use. Since the home crate will also be an important tool in housebreaking, the size of the unit is important.

Many pet owners want to get a crate large enough for the puppy to "grow into" in the interest of saving money. However, when you are housebreaking a dog, you are working with the principle that the animal will not soil its own "den." If you buy a huge crate for a very small dog, the puppy is likely to pick a corner as the "bathroom," thus setting back his training.

Earlier in the book, I gave you a set of target sizes for Cockapoos based on the type of Poodle used to create the mix. Here is that list again, but with recommended crate sizes attached to it.

- Teacup Cockapoos average less than 6 lbs. / 2.72 kg and stand under 10 inches / 25.4 cm. When full grown, this dog should have a crate measuring 19" x 12" x 15" / 48.26 cm x 30.48 cm x 38.1 cm. Average retail cost: $25 / £15.08

- Toy Cockapoos weigh up to 12 lbs. / 5.44 kg, can reach 10 inches / 25.4 cm and tend to have a sturdy build. When full grown, this dog should have a crate measuring 24" x 18" x 20" / 60.96 cm x 45.72 cm x 50.8 cm. Average retail cost: $35 / £21

- Miniature Cockapoos fall in a range of 13-18 lbs. / 5.89-6.35 kg and stand from 11-14 inches / 27.94-35.56 cm. When full grown, this dog should have a crate measuring 24" x 18" x 20" / 60.96 cm x 45.72 cm x 50.8 cm. Average retail cost: $35 / £21

- Standard or Maxi Cockapoos weigh more than 19 lbs. / 8.61 kg and are at least 15 inches / 38.1 cm in stature. When full grown, this dog should have a crate measuring 24" x 18" x 20" / 60.96 cm x 45.72 cm x 50.8 cm. Average retail cost: $35 / £21

For the ride home, put one or two puppy-safe chew toys and an article of clothing you've worn recently in the crate so the dog can begin to "know" you by your scent. Be sure to fasten the seat belt over the crate.

It is best for the puppy not to have had a recent meal and for the dog to have done its "business" prior to being placed in the crate. Coordinate with the breeder to ensure these criteria are met.

Don't be surprised if the puppy whines or cries. Leave it in the crate! It's far safer for the dog to ride there safely buckled in than to be in someone's lap.

If you are driving a considerable distance, some breeders will recommend mild sedation. If you are uncomfortable with this idea, take someone with you to sit next to the crate and comfort the puppy.

Do not, however, overload the dog's senses with too many people. No matter how excited the kids may be at the prospect of a new puppy, leave the children back at the house. The trip home needs to be calm and quiet.

As soon as you arrive home, take the puppy to a patch of grass outside to relieve himself. Immediately begin encouraging him for doing so. Dogs are pack animals with an innate desire to please their "leader." Positive and consistent praise is a very important part of housebreaking.

Even gregarious dogs like Cockapoos will feel nervous in new surroundings. After all, the dog has been taken away from its mother and littermates and all the things that have been a familiar part of its daily life. Do try to stick with the usual feeding schedule, and use the same kind of food that the dog has been receiving in the kennel.

Create a designated "puppy safe" area in the house and let the puppy explore on its own. You don't want the little dog to be isolated, but neither do you want it to be overwhelmed. Absolutely resist the urge to pick up the puppy every time it cries.

Give the little dog soft pieces of worn clothing to further familiarize him with your scent and leave a radio playing softly for "company." At night you may opt to give the baby a well-wrapped warm water bottle, but put the dog in its crate and do not bring it to bed with you.

Now, I realize that last bit may sound all but impossible, however, if you want a crate-trained dog that will stay in its "den" overnight, you have to start from day one. It's much, much harder to get a dog used to sleeping in his crate after he's been allowed any time in the bedroom. You have been warned!

Beyond sleeping arrangements, however, Cockapoos have a recognized tendency for separation anxiety. Crate training is a must with this breed, so you absolutely do not want to engage in behaviors that will undermine this process.

Before you bring your Cockapoo home, you should set aside a certain area in the house as his little zone. This is where you should keep your Cockapoo's crate along with his food and water dishes and toys.

The idea behind this is to provide your Cockapoo with a little place to call his own – a place where he can come to relax and take a nap if he wants to. Ideally, your puppy should come to view his crate as simply a place to sleep and not a form of punishment.

The ideal placement for this area is in a room of the house where your dog will not feel isolated. It shouldn't be in the busiest part of the house either, however.

Once you establish this place, do not move it often – the idea is to give your dog a place where he feels secure and that might not happen if you rearrange things too often.

Go Slow With the Children

If you have children, speak to them in advance of the puppy's arrival, and explain that the little dog will be nervous and a little scared being away from its mother and old home. Help them to understand that during the first few days, the puppy should be handled very gently during limited playtime while everyone is getting to know each other.

In just a matter of days, your Cockapoo puppy will be happily romping with your kids, but this initial transitional time is important. Make sure that your children understand how to safely handle and carry the puppy. All interactions should be monitored for the safety and comfort of all concerned.

Introductions With Other Pets

As I touched on earlier, introductions with other pets, especially with cats, often boil down to an issue of territoriality. All dogs, by nature, defend their territory against intruders, but this is an especially strong instinct in Poodles.

With cats, the best option is to allow for neutral and controlled interaction, as in under a closed bathroom door, before an actual face-to-face encounter. Since cats are "fully weaponized" with an array of razor-sharp claws, Fluffy is usually quite capable of putting a puppy in his place. Of course you want to supervise all such interactions, but it's best to leave the animals to their own devices and not overreact.

With other dogs in the house, however, you may want a more hands-on approach to the first "meet and greet." Always have two people present, so each dog is being controlled. Make the introduction in a place that the older dog does not regard as "his." Even if the two dogs are going to be living in the same house, let them meet in neutral territory.

Keep your tone and demeanor calm, friendly and happy. Let the dogs conduct the usual "sniff test," but don't let it go on for too long as this can be considered aggression by either dog. Puppies, however, may not yet fully understand the behavior of an adult dog and can be absolute little pests.

If this is clearly what is going on, do not scold the older dog for issuing a warning snarl or growl. A well-socialized older dog won't be displaying aggression under such circumstances. He's just putting junior in his place and establishing the hierarchy of the pack.

Be careful when you bring a new dog into the house not to neglect the older dog. Also be sure to spend time with him away from the puppy to assure your existing pet that your bond with him is strong and intact.

Exercise caution at mealtimes, feeding your pets separately so there is no perceived competition for food sources. (This is also a good policy to follow when introducing your puppy to the family cat.)

Common Mistakes to Avoid

Never pick your Cockapoo puppy up if they are showing fear or aggression toward an object, another dog or person, because this will be rewarding them for unbalanced behavior.

If they are doing something you do not want them to continue, your puppy needs to be gently corrected by you with firm and calm energy, so that they learn not to react with fear or aggression. When the mum of the litter tells her puppies off she will use a deep noise with strong eye contact, until the puppy quickly realizes it's doing something naughty.

Don't play the "hand" game, where you slide the puppy across the floor with your hands, because it's amusing for humans to see a little ball of fur scrambling to collect themselves and run back across the floor for another go.

This sort of "game" will teach your puppy to disrespect you as their leader in two different ways — first, because this "game" teaches them that humans are their play toys, and secondly, this type of "game" teaches them that humans are a source of excitement.

When your Cockapoo puppy is teething, they will naturally want to chew on everything within reach, and this will include you. As cute as you might think it is when they are young puppies, this is not an acceptable behavior, and you need to gently, but firmly, discourage the habit, just like a mother dog does to her puppies when they need to be weaned.

Always praise your puppy when they stop inappropriate behavior, as this is the beginning of teaching them to understand rules and boundaries. Often we humans are quick to discipline a puppy or dog for inappropriate behavior, but we forget to praise them for their good behavior.

Don't treat your Cockapoo like a small, furry human. When people try to turn dogs into people, this can cause them much stress and confusion that could lead to behavioral problems.

A well-behaved Cockapoo thrives on rules and boundaries, and when they understand that there is no question you are their leader and they are your follower, they will live a contented, happy and stress-free life.

Dogs are a different species with different rules; for example, they do not naturally cuddle, and they need to learn to be stroked and cuddled by humans. Therefore, be careful when approaching a dog for the first time and being overly expressive with your hands. The safest areas to touch are the back and chest — avoid patting on the head and touching the ears.

Many people will assume that a dog that is yawning is tired — this is often a misinterpretation, and instead it is signaling your dog is uncomfortable and nervous about a situation.

Be careful when staring at dogs because this is one of the ways in which they threaten each other. This body language can make them feel distinctly uneasy.

What Can I Do to Make My Cockapoo Love Me?

From the moment you bring your Cockapoo dog home, every minute you spend with him is an opportunity to bond. The earlier you start working with your dog, the more quickly that bond will grow and the closer you and your Cockapoo will become.

While simply spending time with your Cockapoo will encourage the growth of that bond, there are a few things you can do to purposefully build your bond with your dog. Some of these things include:

•	Taking your Cockapoo for daily walks during which you frequently stop to pet and talk to your dog.

•	Engaging your Cockapoo in games like fetch and hide-and-seek to encourage interaction.

•	Interact with your dog through daily training sessions – teach your dog to pay attention when you say his name.

•	Be calm and consistent when training your dog – always use positive reinforcement rather than punishment.

•	Spend as much time with your Cockapoo as possible, even if it means simply keeping the dog in the room with you while you cook dinner or pay bills.

Puppy Nutrition

As dogs age, they thrive best on a graduated program of nutrition. At age four months and less, puppies should get four small meals a day. From age 4-8 months, three meals per day are appropriate. From 8 months on, feed your pet once or twice a day. Puppies weaned directly onto BARF will only be able to digest 2 or maybe 3 meals a day, as the raw food takes longer to digest.

Cockapoos do have a tendency to become obese if they are not receiving enough exercise. For this reason, I don't recommend the practice of "free feeding," or leaving food (usually dry) out for your pet at all times.

Instead, put the food down for 10-20 minutes. If the dog doesn't eat or only eats part of the serving, you should still take the bowl up at that time and not offer the dog more until the next scheduled feeding.

Photo Credit: Sylvia Hook of Sylml Cockapoo

To give your puppy a good start in life, rely on high-quality, premium dry puppy food. If possible, give the dog whatever it has been used to eating. A sudden dietary switch can cause gastrointestinal upset. Maintain the dog's existing routine if practical.

Before buying any dog food, read the label. The first listed ingredients should be meat, fishmeal or whole grains. Foods with large amounts of fillers like cornmeal or meat by-products have a low nutritional value. They fill your dog up, but they don't give him the range of vitamins and minerals he needs, and they increase the amount of daily waste produced.

Wet foods are typically not appropriate for growing dogs. They do not offer a good nutritional balance, and they are often upsetting to the stomach. Additionally, it's much harder to control portions with wet food, leading to young dogs being over or under fed.

Portion control is an important part of canine husbandry. Give your dog the amount stipulated on the food packaging for his weight and age, and nothing more.

Invest in weighted food and water bowls made out of stainless steel. The weighting prevents the mess of "tip overs," and the material is much easier to clean than plastic, which retains odors and harbors bacteria in scratches and other imperfections.

Bowls in a stand that create a slightly elevated feeding surface are also a good idea, provided your young dog can reach the food and water easily. Typically, stainless steel bowl sets retail for less than $25 / £14.87.

Adult Nutrition

The same basic nutritional guidelines apply to adult Cockapoos. Always start with a high-quality, premium food, preferably a product in the same line as the puppy food you've used.

Graduated product lines help owners to create feeding programs that ensure nutritional consistency. This approach will also allow you to effectively transition your Cockapoo away from puppy food to an adult mixture, and in time to a senior formula according to a recommended schedule. Thankfully, this removes a great deal of the guesswork from the business of nutritional management.

Dogs don't make it easy to say no to them when they beg at the table, but if you let a Cockapoo puppy have so much as that first bite, you've created a little monster – and one with a potentially very unhealthy habit.

Beyond the fact that feeding table scraps contributes to weight problems, many human foods are potentially toxic to dogs. Dangerous items include, but are not limited to:

- Chocolate
- Raisins
- Alcohol
- Human vitamins (especially those with iron)
- Mushrooms
- Onions and garlic
- Walnuts
- Macadamia nuts
- Raw pork

Cockapoos are vigorous chewers, but if you give your puppy a bone, watch him closely. Use only bones that are too large to choke on and take the item away at the first sign of splintering. Frankly, commercial chew toys that are rated "puppy safe" are a much better option.

Treats

Treats are not just for making us guilty humans feel better because we've left our dog home alone for hours, or because it makes us happy to give our pets something they really like. Today's treats are designed to improve our dog's health.

Some of us humans treat our dogs just because, others use treats for training purposes, others for health, while still others treat for a combination of reasons.

Whatever reason you choose to give treats to your Cockapoo, keep in mind that if we treat our dogs too often throughout the day, we may create a picky eater who will no longer want to eat their regular meals.

Plus, if the treats we are giving are high calorie, we may be putting our dog's health in jeopardy by allowing them to become overweight.

Generally, the treats you feed should not make up more than approximately 10% of their daily food intake.

If your Cockapoo will eat them, hard treats will help to keep their teeth cleaner.

Whatever you choose, read the labels and make sure that the ingredients are high quality and appropriately sized for your Cockapoo.

Check any treats to see the country of origin. I would be highly suspect of anything from China, as there have been issues, including deaths from "chicken breast jerky" from China. The large pet store chains in the U.S. have decided to stop carrying many of the Chinese treats.

Soft treats are also available in a wide variety of flavors, shapes and sizes for all the different needs of our furry friends and are often used for training purposes, as they have a stronger smell.

Dental treats or chews are designed with the specific purpose of helping your Cockapoo maintain healthy teeth and gums. They usually require intensive chewing and are often shaped with high ridges and bumps to exercise the jaw and massage gums while removing plaque build-up near the gum line.

The Canine Teeth and Jaw

Even today, far too many dog food choices continue to have far more to do with being convenient for us humans to serve than they do with being a well-balanced, healthy food choice for a canine.

In order to choose the right food for your Cockapoo, first it's important to understand a little bit about canine physiology and what Mother Nature intended when she created our furry companions.

While humans are omnivores who can derive energy from eating plants, our canine companions are carnivores, which means they derive their energy and nutrient requirements from eating a diet consisting mainly or exclusively of the flesh of animals, birds or fish.

Unlike humans, who are equipped with wide, flat molars for grinding grains, vegetables and other plant-based materials, canine teeth are all pointed because they are designed to rip, shred and tear into meat and bone.

Another obvious consideration when choosing an appropriate food source for our furry friends is the fact that every canine is born equipped with powerful jaws and neck muscles for the specific purpose of being able to pull down and tear apart their hunted prey.

The structure of the jaw of every canine is such that it opens widely to hold large pieces of meat and bone, while the mechanics of a dog's jaw permits only vertical (up and down) movement that is designed for crushing.

The Canine Digestive Tract

A dog's digestive tract is short and simple and designed to move their natural choice of food (hide, meat and bone) quickly through their systems.

The canine digestive system is simply unable to properly break down vegetable matter, which is why whole vegetables look pretty much the same going into your dog as they do coming out the other end.

Given the choice, most dogs would never choose to eat plants and grains, or vegetables and fruits over meat, however, we humans continue to feed them a kibble-based diet that contains high amounts of vegetables, fruits and grains with low amounts of meat.

Part of this is because we've been taught that it's a healthy, balanced diet for humans, and therefore, we believe that it must be the same for our dogs, and part of this is because all the fillers that make up our dog's food are less expensive and easier to process than meat.

How much healthier and long lived might our beloved Cockapoo be if, instead of largely ignoring nature's design for our canine companions, we chose to feed them whole, unprocessed, species-appropriate food with the main ingredient being meat?

Whatever you decide to feed your dog, keep in mind that just as too much wheat, other grains and fillers in our human diet is having a detrimental effect on our health, the same can be very true for our best fur friends.

Our dogs are also suffering from many of the same life-threatening diseases that are rampant in our human society as a direct result of consuming a diet high in genetically altered, impure, processed and packaged foods.

The BARF Diet

Raw feeding advocates believe that the ideal diet for their dog is one that would be very similar to what a dog living in the wild would have access to, and these canine guardians are often opposed to feeding their dog any sort of commercially manufactured pet foods.

On the other hand, those opposed to feeding their dogs a raw or Biologically Appropriate Raw Food (BARF) diet believe that the risks associated with food-borne illnesses during the handling and feeding of raw meats outweigh the purported benefits.

Raw meats purchased at your local grocery store contain a much higher level of acceptable bacteria than raw food produced for dogs, because the meat purchased for human consumption is meant to be cooked, which will kill any bacteria.

This means that canine guardians feeding their dogs a raw food diet can be quite certain that commercially prepared raw foods sold in pet stores will be safer than raw meats purchased in grocery stores.

Many guardians of high-energy, working breed dogs will agree that their dogs thrive on a raw or BARF diet and strongly believe that the potential benefits of feeding a dog a raw food diet are many, including:

- Healthy, shiny coats
- Decreased shedding
- Fewer allergy problems
- Healthier skin

- Cleaner teeth
- Fresher breath
- Higher energy levels
- Improved digestion
- Smaller stools
- Strengthened immune system
- Increased mobility in arthritic pets
- General increase or improvement in overall health

All dogs, whether working breed or lap dogs, are amazing athletes in their own right, therefore every dog deserves to be fed the best food available.

A raw diet is a direct evolution of what dogs ate before they became our domesticated pets and we turned toward commercially prepared, easy-to-serve dry dog food that required no special storage or preparation.

The Dehydrated Diet

Dehydrated dog food comes in both raw and cooked forms, and these foods are usually air-dried to reduce moisture to the level where bacterial growth is inhibited.

The appearance of dehydrated dog food is very similar to dry kibble, and the typical feeding methods include adding warm water before serving, which makes this type of diet both healthy for our dogs and convenient for us to serve.

Dehydrated recipes are made from minimally processed fresh whole foods to create a healthy and nutritionally balanced meal that will meet or exceed the dietary requirements for healthy canines.

Dehydrating removes only the moisture from the fresh

ingredients, which usually means that because the food has not already been cooked at a high temperature, more of the overall nutrition is retained.

A dehydrated diet is a convenient way to feed your dog a nutritious diet, because all you have to do is add warm water and wait five minutes while the food re-hydrates so your Cockapoo can enjoy a warm meal.

Photo Credit: Debbie Cowdrey of Starlo's Cockapoos

The Kibble Diet

While many canine guardians are starting to take a closer look at the food choices they are making for their furry companions, there is no mistaking that the convenience and relative economy of dry dog food kibble, which had its beginnings in the 1940s, continues to be the most popular pet food choice for most humans.

While feeding a high-quality, bagged kibble diet that has been flavored to appeal to dogs and supplemented with vegetables and fruits to appeal to humans may keep most every Cockapoo companion happy and healthy, you will need to decide whether this is the best diet for them.

Your Puppy's First Lessons

No young dog should be given full run of the house until it is reliably housetrained. Keep your new pet confined to a designated area behind a baby gate. This not only protects your home and possessions but also keeps the dog safe from potential hazards like staircases. Depending on the size and configuration, baby gates retail from $25-$100 / £14.87-£59.46. During those times when you are not home to supervise the puppy, your pet should be crated.

Housebreaking

Crate training and housebreaking go hand in hand. Cockapoos, like all dogs, quickly come to see their crate as their den. They will hold their need to urinate or defecate while they are inside. Any time you leave the house, you should crate your pet, immediately taking the dog out upon your return.

Establishing and maintaining a daily routine also helps your dog in this respect. Feed your pet at the same time each day, taking him out afterwards. By allowing the feeding schedule to also dictate the frequency of "relief" breaks, these trips "out" will also decrease in number as the dog ages.

Do not, however, hold your puppy strictly to this standard. Puppies have less control over their bladder and bowel movements than adult dogs and will need to go out more often, especially after they have been active or have gotten excited. On average, adult dogs go out 3-4 times a day: when they wake up, within an hour of eating, and right before bedtime. With puppies, however, don't wait more than 15 minutes after a meal.

Consistently praise your pet with the same phrases to encourage and reinforce good elimination habits. NEVER punish a dog for having an accident. There is no association in the dog's mind with the punishment and the incident, so you will do nothing but subject your pet to an uncomfortable, free floating awareness that he's done *something* to make you unhappy.

Of course, if you catch your dog in the act of eliminating in the house, you can and should say "bad dog," but then let the matter go. Clean up the accident using an enzymatic cleaner to eradicate the odor and return to the dog's normal routine.

Nature's Miracle Stain and Odor Removal is an excellent product for this purpose and is very affordable at $5 / £2.97 per 32 ounce / 0.9 liter bottle.

Also good is to go to http://www.removeurineodors.com and order yourself some "SUN" and/or "Max Enzyme," because these products contain professional-strength odor neutralizers and urine digesters that bind to and completely absorb and eliminate odors on any type of surface.

The following are methods that you may or may not have considered, all of which have their own merits, including:

• Bell training
• Exercise pen training
• Free training
• Kennel training

All of these are effective methods, so long as you add in the one critical and often missing "wild card" ingredient, which is "human training."

When you bring home your new Cockapoo puppy, they will be relying upon your guidance to teach them what they need to learn, and when it comes to housetraining, the first thing the human guardian needs to learn is that the puppy is not being bad when they pee or poop inside.

They are just responding to the call of Mother Nature, and you need to pay close attention right from the very beginning, because it's entirely possible to teach a puppy to go to the bathroom outside in less than a week. Therefore, if your puppy is making bathroom "mistakes," blame yourself, not your puppy.

Check in with yourself and make sure your energy remains consistently calm and patient and that you exercise plenty of compassion and understanding while you help your new puppy learn the bathroom rules. Don't clean up after your puppy with them watching, as this makes the puppy believe you are there to clean up after them, making you lower in the dog pack order.

While your puppy is still growing, on average, they can hold it approximately one hour for every month of their age. This means that if your 3-month-old puppy has been happily snoozing for two to three hours, as soon as they wake up, they will need to go outside.

Some of the first indications or signs that your puppy needs to be taken outside to relieve themselves will be when you see them:

• sniffing around
• circling
• looking for the door
• whining, crying or barking
• acting agitated

During the early stages of potty training, adding treats as an extra incentive can be a good way to reinforce how happy you are that your puppy is learning to relieve themselves in the right place. Slowly, treats can be removed and replaced with your happy praise, or you can give your puppy a treat after they are back inside.

Next, now that you have a new puppy in your life, you will want to be flexible with respect to adapting your schedule to meet their internal clocks to quickly teach your Cockapoo puppy their new bathroom routine.

This means not leaving your puppy alone for endless hours at a time, because firstly, they are pack animals that need companionship and your direction at all times, plus long periods alone will result in the disruption of the potty training schedule you have worked hard to establish.

If you have no choice but to leave your puppy alone for many hours, make sure that you place them in a paper-lined room or pen where they can relieve themselves without destroying your newly installed hardwood or favorite carpet.

Remember, your Cockapoo is a growing puppy with a bladder and bowels that they do not yet have complete control over.

Bell Training

A very easy way to introduce your new Cockapoo puppy to house training is to begin by teaching them how to ring a doorbell whenever they need to go outside. A further benefit of training your puppy to ring a bell is that you will not have to listen to your puppy or dog whining, barking or howling to be let out, and your door will not become scratched up from their nails.

Attach the bell to a piece of ribbon or string and hang it from a door handle or tape it to a doorsill near the door where you will be taking your puppy out when they need to relieve themselves. The string will need to be long enough so that your puppy can easily reach the bell with their nose or a paw.

Next, each time you take your puppy out to relieve themselves, say the word "out," and use their paw or their nose to ring the bell. Praise them for this "trick" and immediately take them outside. This type of an alert system is an easy way to eliminate accidents in the home.

Kennel Training

When you train your Cockapoo puppy to accept sleeping in their own kennel at nighttime, this will also help to accelerate their potty training. Because no puppy or dog wants to relieve themselves where they sleep, they will hold their bladder and bowels as long as they possibly can.

Presenting them with familiar scents by taking them to the same spot in the yard or the same street corner will help to remind and encourage them that they are outside to relieve themselves.

Use a voice cue to remind your puppy why they are outside, such as "go pee," and always remember to praise them every time they relieve themselves in the right place, so that they quickly understand what you expect of them.

Exercise Pen Training

The exercise pen is a transition from kennel-only training and will be helpful for those times when you may have to leave your Cockapoo puppy for more hours than they can reasonably be expected to hold it.

Exercise pens are usually constructed of wire sections that you can put together in whatever shape you desire, and the pen needs to be large enough to hold your puppy's kennel in one half of the pen, while the other half will be lined with newspapers or pee pads.

Place your Cockapoo puppy's food and water dishes next to the kennel and leave the kennel door open (or take it off), so they can wander in and out whenever they wish to eat or drink or go to the papers or pee pads if they need to relieve themselves.

Because they are already used to sleeping inside their kennel, they will not want to relieve themselves inside the area where they sleep. Therefore, your puppy will naturally go to the other half of the pen to relieve themselves on the newspapers or pee pads.

Free Training

If you would rather not confine your young Cockapoo puppy to one or two rooms in your home and will be allowing them to freely range about your home anywhere they wish during the day, this is considered free training.

Never get upset or scold a puppy for having an accident inside the home, because this will result in teaching your puppy to be afraid of you and to only relieve themselves in secret places or when you're not watching.

If you catch your Cockapoo puppy making a mistake, all that is necessary is for you to calmly say "no" and quickly scoop them up and take them outside or to their indoor bathroom area.

The Cockapoo is not a difficult puppy to housebreak, and they will generally do very well when you start them off with "puppy pee pads" that you will move closer and closer to the same door that you always use when taking them outside. This way, they will quickly learn to associate going to this door with when they need to relieve themselves.

Photo Credit: Stephen Charlton of Jukee Doodles

Marking Territory

Contrary to popular "wisdom," both male and female dogs with intact reproductive systems will mark territory by urinating. This is most often an outdoor behavior, but can happen inside if the dog is upset about something.

Again, use an enzymatic cleaner to remove the odor. This keeps the dog from being attracted to the same spot again. Since territory marking is especially prevalent in intact males, the obvious long-term solution is to have the dog neutered.

Marking territory is not a consequence of poor housetraining. The behavior can be seen in dogs that would otherwise never "go" in the house and stems from completely different urges and reactions.

Dealing with Separation Anxiety

Separation anxiety manifests in a variety of ways, ranging from vocalizations to nervous chewing. Dogs that are otherwise well trained may urinate or defecate in the house. These behaviors typically begin as soon as your dog recognizes signs that you are leaving, like picking up a set of car keys or putting on a coat. The dog may start to follow you around the house trying to get your attention, jumping up on you or otherwise trying to touch you.

It is imperative that you understand when you adopt a Cockapoo that they are companion dogs. They must have time to connect and be with their humans. You are, literally, the center of your dog's world. The behavior that a dog exhibits when it has separation anxiety is not a case of the animal being "bad." The poor thing misses you terribly and is genuinely distressed.

The purpose of crate training is not to punish or imprison a dog. It is not a cruel or repressive measure. The crate is the dog's "safe place" and is a great coping mechanism for breeds with separation anxiety issues. You are not being mean or cruel teaching your dog to stay in a crate when you are away, you are *helping* your pet to cope.

From the age of 8 weeks old, puppies need rest during the day, rather like human toddlers going down for a sleep. This is an ideal opportunity to place your puppy in its crate that is in the hub of your house, with something pleasant like a chew, a toy, a stuffed Kong, etc. for an hour or so twice a day, say late morning and late afternoon.

While your puppy is resting, vary whether you stay close by and in eye sight of the puppy, whether you move around and go in and out of sight, or whether you sometimes leave the room or house completely for a short while. By mixing up your signals, your dog will quickly learn that all of the above are normal and will accept that as a way of life.

Grooming

Do not allow yourself to get caught in the "my Cockapoo doesn't like it" trap, which is an excuse many owners will use to avoid regular grooming sessions. When you allow your dog to dictate whether they will permit a grooming session, you are setting a dangerous precedent.

Once you have bonded with your dog, they love to be tickled, rubbed and scratched in certain favorite places. This is why grooming is a great source of pleasure and a way to bond with your pet.

It is a misconception to think that just because Cockapoos do not shed a great deal that they don't have to be groomed. Nothing could be further from the truth. Their coats grow very quickly, necessitating regular clipping on a 4-6 week schedule, with brushing several times a week in between to help prevent mats from forming.

- Bristle brushes work well with all coats from long to short, effectively removing dirt and debris and distributing natural oils throughout the coat.

- Wire-pin brushes are for medium to long, curly or wooly

coats and look like a series of pins stuck in a raised base.

- Slicker brushes are excellent for smoothing and detangling, and are especially effective for long hair.

(Note that you can often find combination, two-headed brushes, which will save you a little money and make your grooming sessions more efficient.)

Each of these types of brush is easily acquired for less than $15 / £9 and often less than $10 / £6.

Grooming/brushing sessions are also an excellent opportunity to examine your dog's skin for any growths, lumps, bumps or wounds and to have a good look at his ears, eyes and mouth.

Vigilant prevention is the hallmark of good healthcare for all companion animals. Watch for any discharge from the eyes or ears, as well as evidence of accumulated debris in the ear canal accompanied by a foul or yeasty odor. (This is a sign of parasitical mite activity.)

If you bathe your dog at home in between clippings, do not get your pet's head and ears wet. Clean the dog's head and face with a warm, wet washcloth only. Thoroughly rinse your dog's coat with clean fresh water to remove all residues. Towel your pet dry and make sure he doesn't get chilled.

Although some brave owners may clip their dogs at home, I recommend using the services of a professional. The risk of injuring your dog with a cutting implement is too great in my opinion, and most groomers are quite reasonable, charging in a range of $25-$50 / £15-£30 per session.

How to Bathe Your Cockapoo

The earlier you start bathing your Cockapoo, the easier it is going to be – if your Cockapoo gets used to it as a puppy then he will be less difficult to handle later. Follow the tips below to bathe your Cockapoo:

1.) Fill a bathtub with several inches of warm water – make sure it is not too hot.
2.) Place your Cockapoo in the tub and wet down his coat.
3.) Apply a dollop of dog shampoo to your hands and work it into your Cockapoo's coat, starting at the base of his neck.
4.) Work the shampoo into your dog's back and down his legs and tail.
5.) Rinse your dog well, making sure to get rid of all the soap.
6.) Towel dry your Cockapoo to remove as much moisture as possible.
7.) If desired, use a hair dryer on the cool setting to dry your Cockapoo's coat the rest of the way.

It is very important that you avoid getting water in your Cockapoo's ears and eyes. If your Cockapoo's ears get wet, dry them carefully with a cotton ball to prevent infection.

Nail Trimming

Coat maintenance is not the only grooming chore necessary to keep your Cockapoo in good shape. Even dogs that routinely walk on asphalt or other rough surfaces will need to have their nails trimmed from time to time.

If your dog is agreeable, this is a job you can perform at home with a trimmer especially designed for use with dogs. I prefer those with plier grips. They're easier to handle and quite cost effective, selling for under $20 / £11.88.

Snip off the nail tips at a 45-degree angle, being careful not to cut too far down. If you do, you'll catch the vascular quick, which will hurt the dog and bleed profusely. If you are apprehensive about performing this chore, ask your vet tech or groomer to walk you through it the first time.

Anal Glands

All dogs can suffer from blocked anal glands, typically indicated by the dog scooting or rubbing its bottom on the ground or carpet. (You may also notice a foul odor.)

If this occurs, the glands will need to be expressed to prevent an abscess from forming. This is a sensitive task and one that a veterinarian or a highly experienced groomer should perform.

Fleas

I'm including fleas and ticks under grooming because both are typically discovered by and addressed through grooming sessions. Don't think that if your Cockapoo suddenly has "passengers" you're doing something wrong, or that the dog is at fault. This is simply a part of dog ownership. Sooner or later, it will happen. Of course the problem needs to be dealt with immediately, but it's not a reason to "freak out."

Do NOT use a commercial flea product on a puppy of less than 12 weeks of age and be extremely careful with adult dogs. Most of the major products contain pyrethrum. This chemical has been responsible for adverse reactions, including long-term neurological damage and even fatalities in small dogs.

To get rid of fleas, bathe your dog in warm water with a

standard canine shampoo. Comb the animal's fur with a fine-toothed flea comb, which will trap the live parasites. Repeatedly submerge the comb in hot soapy water to kill the fleas.

Wash all of the dog's bedding and any soft materials with which he has come in contact. Look for any accumulations of "flea dirt," which is excreted blood from adult fleas. Wash the bedding and other surfaces daily for at least a week to kill any remaining eggs before they hatch.

If you find a tick, coat it with a thick layer of petroleum jelly for 5 minutes to suffocate the parasite and cause its jaws to release. Pluck the tick off with a pair of tweezers using a straight motion. Never just jerk a tick off a dog. The parasite's head will be left behind and will continue to burrow into the skin, making a painful sore.

Managing Your Active Cockapoo

Your Cockapoo will be up for almost any outing you propose,

including jumping in the nearest body of water for a swim. They love all kinds of exercise and play. Clearly, unless you are in an area where your dog can run free, he will have to be wearing a collar or harness and be on a leash.

If you have a fenced yard where your dog can run around, that is great, but it shouldn't be viewed as a substitute for taking your dog on a walk at least once a day.

Collar or Harness?

Regardless of breed, I'm not a big fan of using a traditional collar for the simple reason that I wouldn't enjoy a choking sensation and assume my dog wouldn't either. My current favorite on-body restraints are the harnesses that look like vests that offer a point of attachment for the lead on the back between the shoulders.

This arrangement directs pressure away from the neck and allows for easy, free movement. Young dogs are considerably less resistant to this system and don't strain against a harness the way they will with a collar.

It's best to take your dog with you to the pet store to get a proper fit. Sizing for a dog is much more unpredictable than you might think. I have seen dogs as large as 14 lbs. / 6.35 kg require an "Extra Small" depending on their build.

Regardless of size, however, harnesses retail in a range of $20 - $25 / £11.88 - £14.85.

The decision to buy a standard, fixed-length leash or a retractable lead is, for the most part, a matter of personal preference. Some facilities like groomers, vet clinics and dog daycares ask that you not use a retractable lead on their premises, as the long line represents a trip and fall hazard for other human clients.

Fixed-length leashes often sell for as little as $5 / £2.97, while retractable leads are generally less than $15 / £8.91.

Learning to respond to your control of the leash is an important behavioral lesson for your Cockapoo. Do not drag a dog on a lead or jerk him. If your pet stubbornly sits down and refuses to budge, pick him up. Don't let the dog be in charge of the walk or you'll have the devil's own time regaining the upper hand.

Cockapoos are so intelligent that they immediately come to associate the lead with adventures and outings with their human, a huge positive in their book.

Don't be at all surprised if your dog picks up words associated with excursions like go, out, car, drive or walk. Many Cockapoos have been known to pick up their leash and bring it to their humans when they hear one of these words.

Dog Walking Tips

Active dogs like Cockapoos are so "into" the whole walking experience that this is an excellent opportunity to use the activity to build and reinforce good behaviors on command.

Teach your dog to "sit" by using the word and making a downward pointing motion with your finger or the palm of your hand. Do not attach the lead until your dog complies, rewarding his patience with the words he most wants to hear, "Okay, let's go!"

If your dog jerks or pulls on the leash, stop, pick up the dog and start the walk over with the "sit" command. Make it clear that the walk ceases when the dog misbehaves.

Praise your dog for walking well on the end of the lead and for stopping when you stop. The more that you can reinforce positive behaviors as part of the shared walking experience, the more the dog will exhibit those same behaviors in other aspects of your activities together.

Photo Credit: Jamie of Cute Cockapoos

Your dog's main sense is scent, which is why when you take them for a walk they spend a lot of time sniffing everything. They gather an amazing amount of information, such as being able to determine which dogs were recently in the area, their gender, their current health and age.

When two dogs meet they are likely to go up to each other and sniff near each other's jaw and then around the rear-end area.

Have you ever visited a friend and their dog has come up to you and sniffed your groin area? This may have caused some embarrassment, but this is simply a dog's way of learning about you by picking up scents.

The Importance of Basic Commands

It is greatly to your advantage to go through a basic obedience class with your dog. By their very nature, canines are eager to please, but they require direction. Much of this lies simply in a consistent routine and command "language."

Experts agree that most dogs can pick up between 165 and 200 words, but they can't extrapolate multiple meanings. If, for instance, your dog barks, you need to use the same "command" in response, like "quiet."

If he picks something up, you might say "drop it." For problem jumping, most owners go with "down." The point, however, is to pick a set of words and use them over and over again to create a basic vocabulary for your dog. Both the word and your tone of voice should convey your authority and elicit the desired response.

This is not a difficult process with a breed whose native intelligence is as advanced as that of the Cockapoo. Investigate enrollment in on obedience class through your local big box pet store or by asking your vet about trainers in your area, but start the lessons early in your dog's life by simply offering him the stability of consistent reactions on your part.

Play Time and Tricks

Cockapoos have a reputation for being highly trainable dogs. If you show them something once, like shaking hands or rolling over, they immediately seem to understand what you want them to do and may even add a creative twist of their own making. It's always a good idea to cater to some natural tendency the dog exhibits to "teach" the first trick and then extrapolate from there.

Always offer praise and show pleasure for correct responses. This makes training just another form of play – and Cockapoos love to play. You'll be shocked at how quickly your dog amasses a collection of toys, or how rapidly your pet's enthusiastic chewing destroys many of them.

Playtime is important, especially for a dog's natural desire to chase. Try channeling this instinct with toys and games. If a dog has no stimulation and has nothing to chase, they can start to chase their own tail, which can lead to problems.

Toys can be used to simulate the dog's natural desire to hunt. For example, when they catch a toy, they will often shake it and bury their teeth into it, simulating the killing of their prey.

Allow your dog to fulfill a natural desire to chew. This comes from historically catching their prey and then chewing the carcass. Providing chews or bones can prevent your dog from destroying your home.

Playing with your dog is not only a great way of getting them to use up their energy, but it is also a great way of bonding with them as they have fun. Dogs love to chase and catch balls, just make sure that the ball is too large to be swallowed.

Deer antlers are wonderful toys for Cockapoos. Most love them. They do not smell, are all-natural and do not stain or splinter. I recommend the antlers that are not split as they last longer.

Don't select toys that are soft and "shred-able." I recommend chew toys like Nylabones that can withstand the abuse. Items made out of this tough material cost about $1-$5 / £0.59-£2.97.

Never give your dog rawhide, cow hooves or pig's ears. The rawhide and pig's ears become soft and present choking hazards;

the cow hooves splinter and can puncture the cheek or palate.

Avoid soft rubber toys that can be pulverized into pieces, which the dog will swallow. Opt for rope toys instead. Don't buy anything with a squeaker or any other part that presents a choking hazard.

Dogs that don't get enough exercise are also more likely to develop problem behaviors like chewing, digging and barking.

Tips for giving your Cockapoo extra exercise:

• Play a game of tug-of-war with your dog in the house.

• Engage your dog in a game of hide-and-seek.

• Play fetch with your dog outside in the back yard.

• Take your Cockapoo to the dog park.

Photo Credit: Jackie Stafford of Dj's Cockapoo Babies

Chapter 6 - Training and Problem Behaviors

Training starts from the minute you bring your Cockapoo puppy home. You may not realize it, but everything you do teaches your Cockapoo puppy how to act. Many dog owners make the mistake of giving their puppy free reign for the first few weeks, and then they are surprised when it comes time for training and the puppy has already developed hard-to-break habits.

Photo Credit: Stephen Charlton of Jukee Doodles

If you want to raise a well-trained and obedient dog, you should start your training early by rewarding your puppy for doing the things you want him to do and discouraging him from unwanted behaviors.

Although Cockapoos are typically not aggressive or ill-tempered dogs, they can, like any dog, exhibit poor or ill-tempered behaviors, be high strung or be possessive about their perceived territory and human companions. This behavior may not be directed toward humans, but might be reserved for other dogs through such actions as snapping, lunging, pushing, barking or baring of the teeth.

Most if not all of these potential problem behaviors can be overcome with proper socialization that starts at a young age. Taking your puppy to a training class will help to introduce him to new sights, sounds, people and places as well as letting him interact with other dogs in a controlled environment.

In such an environment, the dog is safe to deal with fear and timidity around other dogs, with no need to bluster in self-defense. The result is not only a better-mannered dog, but a greater understanding on your part of how to guide your dog's interactions.

As a responsible dog owner, you must remain constantly attentive not just of your dog's behavior, but to what is going on in the world around you. Praise your dog when he behaves well, but realize that you, too, bear a responsibility in forestalling potential clashes. Often in a public setting, the wisest course of action is to avoid a meeting with another dog altogether, especially if the other dog is exhibiting warning signs of being "bad."

In the last chapter, I discussed leash training, which is crucial for successful public outings. Rather than avoiding areas with other people and dogs, your goal is to be able to take your dog to such places without incident.

Cockapoos thrive on interaction and will be happily engaged in interesting public places like parks, walking trails or beaches that are full of new sights, sounds and smells. Contrary to what some people think, well-managed outings in varied environments help to create confidence in your dog.

Dog Whispering

Many people can be confused when they need professional help with their dog, because for many years, if you needed help with your dog, you contacted a "dog trainer" or took your dog to "puppy classes" where your dog would learn how to sit or stay.

The difference between a dog trainer and a dog whisperer would be that a "dog trainer" teaches a dog how to perform certain tasks, and a "dog whisperer" alleviates behavior problems by teaching humans what they need to do to keep their particular dog happy.

Often, depending on how soon the guardian has sought help, this can mean that the dog in question has developed some pretty serious issues, such as aggressive barking, lunging, biting or attacking other dogs, pets or people.

Dog whispering is often an emotional roller coaster ride for the humans involved that unveils many truths when they finally realize that it has been their actions (or inactions) that have likely caused the unbalanced behavior that their dog is now displaying.

Once solutions are provided, the relief for both dog and human can be quite cathartic when they realize that with the correct direction, they can indeed live a happy life with their dog.

All specific methods of training, such as "clicker training," fall outside of what every dog needs to be happy, because training your dog to respond to a clicker, which you can easily do on your own, and then letting them sleep in your bed, eat from your plate and any other multitude of things humans allow, are what makes the dog unbalanced and causes behavior problems.

I always say to people, don't wait until you have a severe problem before getting some dog whispering or professional help of some sort, because "With the proper training, Man can learn to be dog's best friend."

Photo Credit: Ali Haynes of Tiddybrook Cockapoos

Rewarding Unwanted Behavior

It is very important to recognize that any attention paid to an out-of-control, adolescent puppy, even negative attention, is likely to be exciting and rewarding for your Cockapoo puppy.

Chasing after a puppy when they have taken something they shouldn't have, picking them up when barking or showing aggression, pushing them off when they jump on other people, or yelling when they refuse to come when called are all forms of attention that can actually be rewarding for most puppies.

It will be your responsibility to provide structure for your puppy, which will include finding acceptable and safe ways to allow your puppy to vent their energy without being destructive or harmful to others.

The worst thing you can do when training your Cockapoo is to yell at him or use punishment. Positive reinforcement training methods – that is, rewarding your dog for good behavior – are infinitely more effective than negative reinforcement – training by punishment.

It is important when training your Cockapoo that you do not allow yourself to get frustrated. If you feel yourself starting to get angry, take a break and come back to the training session later.

Why is punishment-based training so bad? Think about it this way – your dog should listen to you because he wants to please you, right?

If you train your dog using punishment, he could become fearful of you and that could put a damper on your relationship with him. Do your dog and yourself a favor by using positive reinforcement.

Teaching Basic Commands

When it comes to training your Cockapoo, you have to start off slowly with the basic commands. The most popular basic commands for dogs include sit, down, stay and come.

Sit

This is the most basic and one of the most important commands you can teach your Cockapoo.

1.)   Stand in front of your Cockapoo with a few small treats in your pocket.

2.)   Hold one treat in your dominant hand and wave it in front of your Cockapoo's nose so he gets the scent.

3.)   Give the "Sit" command.

4.)   Move the treat upward and backward over your Cockapoo's head so he is forced to raise his head to follow it.

5.)   In the process, his bottom will lower to the ground.

6.)   As soon as your Cockapoo's bottom hits the ground, praise him and give him the treat.

7.)   Repeat this process several times until your dog gets the hang of it and responds consistently.

Down

After the "Sit" command, "Down" is the next logical command to teach because it is a progression from "Sit."

1.)   Kneel in front of your Cockapoo with a few small treats in your pocket.

2.)   Hold one treat in your dominant hand and give your Cockapoo the "Sit" command.

3.)   Reward your Cockapoo for sitting, then give him the "Down" command.

4.)   Quickly move the treat down to the floor between your Cockapoo's paws.

5.)   Your dog will follow the treat and should lie down to retrieve it.

6.)   Praise and reward your Cockapoo when he lies down.

7.)   Repeat this process several times until your dog gets the hang of it and responds consistently.

Photo Credit: Shannon Wallace of OZ Cockapoos

Come

It is very important that your Cockapoo responds to a "come" command, because there may come a time when you need to get his attention and call him to your side during a dangerous situation (such as him running around too close to traffic).

1.)   Put your Cockapoo on a short leash and stand in front of him.

2.) Give your Cockapoo the "come" command, then quickly take a few steps backward away from him.

3.) Clap your hands and act excited, but do not repeat the "come" command.

4.) Keep moving backwards in small steps until your Cockapoo follows and comes to you.

5.) Praise and reward your Cockapoo and repeat the process.

6.) Over time you can use a longer leash or take your Cockapoo off the leash entirely.

7.) You can also start by standing further from your Cockapoo when you give the "come" command.

8.) If your Cockapoo doesn't come to you immediately, you can use the leash to pull him toward you.

Stay

This command is very important because it teaches your Cockapoo discipline – not only does it teach your Cockapoo to stay, but it also forces him to listen and pay attention to you.

1.) Find a friend to help you with this training session.

2.) Have your friend hold your Cockapoo on the leash while you stand in front of the dog.

3.) Give your Cockapoo the "sit" command and reward him for responding correctly.

4.)   Give your dog the "stay" command while holding your hand out like a "stop" sign.

5.)   Take a few steps backward away from your dog and pause for 1 to 2 seconds.

6.)   Step back toward your Cockapoo, then praise and reward your dog.

7.)   Repeat the process several times, then start moving back a little further before you return to your dog.

Beyond Basic Training

Once your Cockapoo has a firm grasp on the basics, you can move on to teaching him additional commands. You can also add distractions to the equation to reinforce your dog's mastery of the commands. The end goal is to ensure that your Cockapoo responds to your command each and every time – regardless of distractions and anything else he might rather be doing. This is incredibly important, because there may come a time when your dog is in a dangerous situation and if he doesn't respond to your command, he could get hurt.

After your Cockapoo has started to respond correctly to the basic commands on a regular basis, you can start to incorporate distractions.

If you previously conducted your training sessions indoors, you might consider moving them outside where your dog could be distracted by various sights, smells and sounds.

One thing you might try is to give your dog the Stay command and then toss a toy nearby that will tempt him to break his Stay.

Start by tossing the toy at a good distance from him and wait a few seconds before you release him to play.

Eventually you will be able to toss a toy right next to your dog without him breaking his Stay until you give him permission to do so.

Incorporating Hand Signals

Teaching your Cockapoo to respond to hand signals in addition to verbal commands is very useful – you never know when you will be in a situation where your dog might not be able to hear you.

To start out, choose your dominant hand to give the hand signals, and hold a small treat in that hand while you are training your dog – this will encourage your dog to focus on your hand during training, and it will help to cement the connection between the command and the hand signal.

To begin, give your dog the Sit or Down command while holding the treat in your dominant hand and give the appropriate hand signal – for Sit you might try a closed fist and, for Down, you might place your hand flat, parallel to the ground.

When your dog responds correctly, give him the treat. You will need to repeat this process many times in order for your dog to form a connection between both the verbal command and the hand signal with the desired behavior.

Eventually, you can start to remove the verbal command from the equation – use the hand gesture every time, but start to use the verbal command only half the time.

Once your dog gets the hang of this, you should start to remove the food reward from the equation. Continue to give your dog the hand signal for each command, and occasionally use the verbal command just to remind him.

You should start to phase out the food rewards, however, by offering them only half the time. Progressively lessen the use of the food reward, but continue to praise your dog for performing the behavior correctly so he learns to repeat it.

Teaching Distance Commands

In addition to getting your dog to respond to hand signals, it is also useful to teach him to respond to your commands even when you are not directly next to him.

This may come in handy if your dog is running around outside and gets too close to the street – you should be able to give him a Sit or Down command so he stops before he gets into a dangerous situation.

Teaching your dog distance commands is not difficult, but it does require some time and patience.

To start, give your Cockapoo a brief refresher course of the basic commands while you are standing or kneeling right next to him.

Next, give your dog the Sit and Stay commands, then move a few feet away before you give the Come command.

Repeat this process, increasing the distance between you and your dog before giving him the Come command. Be sure to praise and reward your dog for responding appropriately when he does so.

Once your dog gets the hang of coming on command from a distance, you can start to incorporate other commands.

One method of doing so is to teach your dog to sit when you grab his collar. To do so, let your dog wander freely and every once in a while walk up and grab his collar while giving the Sit command.

After a few repetitions, your dog should begin to respond with a Sit when you grab his collar, even if you do not give the command.

Gradually, you can increase the distance from which you come to grab his collar and give him the command.

After your dog starts to respond consistently when you come from a distance to grab his collar, you can start giving the Sit command without moving toward him.

It may take your dog a few times to get the hang of it, so be patient. If your dog doesn't Sit right away, calmly walk up to him and repeat the Sit command, but do not grab his collar this time.

Eventually, your dog will get the hang of it, and you can start to practice using other commands like Down and Stay from a distance.

Clicker Training

When it comes to training your Cockapoo, you are going to be most successful if you maintain consistency. Cockapoos have a tendency to be a little stubborn, so unless you are very clear with your dog about what your expectations are, he may simply decide not to follow your commands.

A simple way to achieve consistency in training your Cockapoo is to use the principles of clicker training. Clicker training involves using a small handheld device that makes a clicking noise when you press it between your fingers.

Clicker training is based on the theory of operant conditioning, which helps your dog to make the connection between the desired behavior and the offering of a reward.

Cockapoos have a natural desire to please, so if they learn that a certain behavior earns your approval, they will be eager to repeat it – clicker training is a great way to help your dog quickly identify the particular behavior you want him to repeat.

All you have to do is give your Cockapoo a command and, as soon as he performs the behavior, you use the clicker. After you use the clicker, give your dog the reward as you would with any form of positive reinforcement training.

Some of the benefits of clicker training include:

• Very easy to implement – all you need is the clicker.

• Helps your dog form a connection between the command and the desired behavior more quickly.

• You only need to use the clicker until your dog makes the connection, then you can stop.

• May help to keep your dog's attention more effectively if he hears the noise.

Clicker training is just one method of positive reinforcement training that you can consider for training your Cockapoo.

No matter what method you choose, it is important that you maintain consistency and always praise and reward your dog for responding to your commands correctly so he learns to repeat the behavior.

Photo Credit: Joanna Johnson

First Tricks

When teaching your Cockapoo their first tricks, in order to give them extra incentive, find a small treat that they would do anything to get, and give the treat as a reward to help solidify a good performance.

Most dogs will be extra attentive during training sessions when they know that they will be rewarded with their favorite treats.

If your Cockapoo is less than six months old when you begin teaching them tricks, keep your training sessions short (no more than 5 or 10 minutes) and make the sessions lots of fun.

As your Cockapoo becomes an adult, you can extend your sessions, because they will be able to maintain their focus for longer periods of time.

Shake a Paw

Who doesn't love a dog who knows how to shake a paw? This is one of the easiest tricks to teach your Cockapoo.

Practice every day until they are 100% reliable with this trick, and then it will be time to add another trick to their repertoire.

Most dogs are naturally either right or left pawed. If you know which paw your dog favors, ask them to shake this paw.

Find a quiet place to practice, without noisy distractions or other pets, and stand or sit in front of your dog. Place them in the sitting position and hold a treat in your left hand.

Say the command "Shake" while putting your right hand behind their left or right paw and pulling the paw gently toward yourself until you are holding their paw in your hand. Immediately praise them and give them the treat.

Most dogs will learn the "Shake" trick very quickly, and in no time at all, once you put out your hand, your Cockapoo will immediately lift their paw and put it into your hand, without your assistance or any verbal cue.

Roll Over

You will find that just like your Cockapoo is naturally either right or left pawed, that they will also naturally want to roll either to the right or the left side.

Take advantage of this by asking your dog to roll to the side they naturally prefer. Sit with your dog on the floor and put them in a lie down position.

Hold a treat in your hand and place it close to their nose without allowing them to grab it, and while they are in the lying position, move the treat to the right or left side of their head so that they have to roll over to get to it.

You will quickly see which side they want to naturally roll to; once you see this, move the treat to that side. Once they roll over to that side, immediately give them the treat and praise them.

You can say the verbal cue "Over" while you demonstrate the hand signal motion (moving your right hand in a half circular motion) from one side of their head to the other.

Sit Pretty

While this trick is a little more complicated, and most dogs pick up on it very quickly, remember that this trick requires balance, and every dog is different, so always exercise patience.

Find a quiet space with few distractions and sit or stand in front of your dog and ask them to "Sit."

Have a treat nearby (on a countertop or table) and when they sit, use both of your hands to lift up their front paws into the sitting pretty position, while saying the command "Sit Pretty." Help them balance in this position while you praise them and give them the treat.

Once your Cockapoo can do the balancing part of the trick quite easily without your help, sit or stand in front of your dog while asking them to "Sit Pretty" and hold the treat above their head, at the level their nose would be when they sit pretty.

If they attempt to stand on their back legs to get the treat, you may be holding the treat too high, which will encourage them to stand up on their back legs to reach it. Go back to the first step and put them back into the "Sit" position and again lift their paws while their backside remains on the floor.

The hand signal for "Sit Pretty" is a straight arm held over your dog's head with a closed fist. Place your Cockapoo beside a wall when first teaching this trick so that they can use the wall to help their balance.

A young Cockapoo puppy should be able to easily learn these basic tricks before they are six months old, and when you are patient and make your training sessions short and fun for your dog, they will be eager to learn more.

Excessive Jumping

Thanks to the Poodle blood coursing in their veins, Cockapoos are the super-dog jumpers of the canine world. Unfortunately, they can also get completely out of control, knocking things and people over and scratching you and your visitors in their exuberant enthusiasm. This is, however, one of the most undesirable of all traits in an uncontrolled dog, especially if the dog has muddy paws or is meeting a frail individual with poor balance. Many people are also afraid of dogs and find spontaneous jumping frightening and threatening.

Don't make the mistake of assuming that excessive jumping is an expression of friendliness. All too often, it's a case of a dominant dog asserting his authority and saying basically, "I don't respect you." Dogs that know their proper place in the "pack" don't jump on more dominant dogs. Therefore, a jumper sees himself as the "top dog" in all situations.

Regardless of the reaction of the person in question, however, you, as the dog's master, must consistently enforce the "no jumping" rule. Anything else will only confuse your pet. Dogs have a keen perception of space. Rather than retreating from a jumping dog, step sideways and forward, taking back your space that he is trying to claim.

You are not trying to knock your dog down, but don't be overly concerned if the dog careens into you and falls down. Remain casual and calm, not moving rapidly, but protecting a "bubble" around your body. Your dog won't be expecting this action from you and won't enjoy being thrown off balance.

It may take several failed jumps, but in time, your dog won't think jumping on you is nearly as much fun anymore, because his dominant message is no longer getting across.

Barking Behavior

Excessive barking is a serious problem behavior, especially when you live in close proximity to other people. If you are in an apartment complex with shared walls, a barking dog can easily get you thrown out of your home. To get to the bottom of problem barking, you must first try to figure out what is setting your dog off. Is he lonely? Bored? Wanting attention? Overly excited? Anxious? Is he responding to something he's seeing? Hearing? Smelling?

As with all problem behaviors, patience and consistency are needed to address problem barking. If a firm "No" or "Quiet" fails to work, try spraying your dog with water from a mister or squirt gun. Aim for the face. You won't hurt your pet, but you will get his attention. (Do be careful about your pet's eyes.)

For real problem barkers, there are now humane bark collars that will teach the dog through negative reinforcement. These collars, rather than delivering a cruel electric shock, shoot a spray of harmless citronella into the dog's nose in response to vibrations in the throat. The system, though somewhat expensive at $100/£60, works very rapidly in almost all cases.

Chewing

Chewing is a natural behavior in dogs that must be directed to prevent damage and destruction in the home. Excessive chewing indicates some combination of anxiety or boredom, which may mean you need to get your dog out of the house more.

Regardless, however, make sure that your dog has proper chew toys, like Nylabones, that exist to be destroyed! If you catch your pet chewing on a forbidden object, quickly reprimand him and take the item away, immediately substituting it with an appropriate chew toy.

Digging

Thanks to their hunting heritage, derived from both foundation breeds, Cockapoos love to dig. Indoors, this behavior, like barking and chewing, can be an expression of fear, anxiety and/or boredom. Because the breed is also prone to separation anxiety, the Cockapoo may well be trying to dig his way out to come find you.

Digging is a very difficult behavior to control and one that can be highly destructive if the dog has decided to go after the sofa or some other piece of furniture. The best solution is to spend more time playing with and exercising your pet. Also, consider enrolling your pet in a dog daycare facility, so he will not be alone while you are at work.

Photo Credit: Jessica Sampson of Legacy Cockapoos

Begging

As I discussed in the section on nutrition, Cockapoos can develop weight problems if they do not get enough exercise and if they are allowed to beg from the table and eat human food. My best advice to you is to never allow this behavior to get started by making "people" food off limits from day one.

If, however, your pet becomes a serious beggar, confine him to another part of the house during meal times. Frankly, this is as much a control measure for you and other people at the table who don't have the fortitude to ignore a plaintive, begging set of Cockapoo eyes!

Chasing

Cockapoos are excellent runners and all too likely to give into their natural instinct to chase things. Clearly this can be an enormous danger to your dog if he is not properly restrained. When you are out with your dog, especially near busy urban areas, you must keep your pet leashed at all times. Never allow your dog off the leash unless you are in a fenced, completely secure area. Many dogs become so intent on the chase they will not come when they are called.

Biting

It is extremely rare for a Cockapoo to exhibit problem biting. Puppies will nip and bite when they play, a behavior that should be gently curbed before it becomes a problem.

Any dog will bite, however, if he is reacting out of pain or fear. Biting is a primary means of defense. Controlling a puppy's playful nips is a matter of socialization, obedience training and stern corrections.

If an adult dog displays biting behavior, it is imperative to get to the bottom of the biting, including having the dog evaluated for a health problem and working with a professional trainer. Again, this is an extremely rare concern with Cockapoos.

Chapter 7 – Cockapoo Dog Health

You are, in essence, your Cockapoo's primary healthcare provider. You are the one who will know what is "normal" for your dog, and yours will be the best sense that something is "wrong," even when there is no obvious injury or illness. The more that you understand about the fundamentals of preventive health care, the better you will be able to care for your dog throughout his life.

Photo Credit: Stephen Charlton of Jukee Doodles

Your Veterinarian Is Your Partner

Working with a qualified veterinarian is critical to long-term and comprehensive healthcare for a companion animal. If you do not already have a vet, ask your breeder for a recommendation. If you purchased your pet outside your area, contact your local dog club and ask for referrals.

Make an appointment to tour the clinic and meet the vet. Be clear about the purpose of your visit and about your intent to pay the regular office fee. Don't expect to get a freebie interview, and don't waste anyone's time! Go in with a set of prepared questions. Be sure to cover the following points:

- How long has this practice been in operation?
- How many vets are on staff?
- Are any of your doctors specialists?
- What are your regular business hours?
- Do you recommend a specific emergency clinic?
- Do you have emergency hours?
- What specific medical services do you offer?
- Do you offer grooming services?
- May I have an estimated schedule of fees?
- Do you currently treat any Cockapoos?

Pay attention to all aspects of your visit, including how the facilities appear and demeanor of the staff. Things to look for:

- how the staff interacts with clients
- the degree of organization or lack thereof
- indications of engagement with the clientele (office bulletin board, cards and photos displayed, etc.)
- quality of all visible equipment
- cleanliness and orderliness of the waiting area and back rooms
- prominent display of doctors' credentials

These are only some suggestions. Go with your "gut." If the clinic and staff seems to "feel" right to you, trust your instincts. If not, no matter how well appointed the practice may appear to be, visit more clinics before making a decision.

First Visit to the Vet

When you are sufficiently comfortable with a practice and

veterinarian, schedule a second visit that will include your Cockapoo puppy. Bring all the dog's medical records with you, and be prepared to discuss completing the required vaccinations and having the animal spayed or neutered.

Routine examination procedures include temperature and a check of heart and lung function with a stethoscope. The puppy will be weighed and measured to provide baseline figures by which growth rate and physical progress may be judged. If you have specific questions about your dog's healthcare moving forward, prepare them in advance.

Vaccinations

A puppy's normally recommended vaccinations begin at 6-7 weeks of age. The first injection covers distemper, hepatitis, parvovirus, parainfluenza and coronavirus.

Recommended boosters are given at 9, 12 and 16 weeks. In some geographical regions, a vaccine for Lyme disease may be started at 16 weeks with a booster at 18 weeks.

The rabies vaccination is administered at 12-16 weeks and annually for life thereafter.

Evaluating for Worms

It is standard procedure for the owner of a new puppy to be asked to collect a fresh stool sample before the first vet visit. The fecal matter will be tested for parasites, which can be easily eradicated with an initial dose of a deworming agent and a follow-up treatment in 10 days.

Although it is unlikely that a puppy purchased from a breeder will have parasites, such infestations are more common in rescue dogs. Roundworms will appear as small white granules around the anus, while the presence of other types of worms must be verified through microscopic examination. These are important tests, however, since some parasites, like tapeworms, may be life threatening.

Spaying and Neutering

In cases of purebred adoptions, spaying and neutering before six months of age is generally required under the adoption agreement. In crossbreeds like the Cockapoo, owners are faced with making the decision on their own. I recommend that you move forward with either procedure not only to eliminate unwanted pregnancies, but also for the significant associated health benefits for your pet.

Neutering reduces the risk of prostatic disease or perianal tumors in male dogs while lessening aggressive behaviors and territorial instincts, which in turn lowers the chance of urine marking or inappropriate mounting. Spayed females have a diminished risk for breast cancer and no prospect of uterine or ovarian cancer. There are no hormonally related mood swings or issues around the dog coming into season.

"Normal" Health Issues

Although Cockapoos are generally exuberantly happy, hardy dogs, they, like all canines, can face health issues. The following are some of the more "normal" health-related matters that may come up in a dog's life and can, at the very least, require evaluation by a vet.

Any time that your normally energetic Cockapoo seems inattentive or lethargic and stops eating or drinking water, seek medical attention for your pet immediately. This is definitely

NOT normal behavior for the breed.

Photo Credit: Stephen Charlton of Jukee Doodles

Diarrhea

Cockapoo puppies are easily subject to digestive upsets, often because they've gotten into something they shouldn't have, like human food or even the kitchen garbage. Instances of diarrhea attributable to these sorts of causes will generally resolve spontaneously within 24 hours.

During that time, the puppy should have only small portions of dry food and no treats. Give the dog lots of fresh, clean water to guard against dehydration. If the loose, watery stools are still present after 24 hours, take your Cockapoo to the vet.

The same period of watchful waiting for adult dogs with diarrhea applies, but if the condition becomes chronically episodic, it's time to take a good hard look at your pet's diet.

Chances are good the dog is getting too much rich, fatty food and needs a mixture lower in both fat and protein. Some dogs also do better eating small amounts of food multiple times a day rather than having 2-3 larger meals.

Some cases of diarrhea are linked to allergies, which can be pinpointed with testing. Many smaller dogs are allergic to chicken and turkey. Their gastrointestinal upset clears up immediately when they are switched to a different meat-based food, for instance one that includes rabbit or duck.

Either a bacteria or a virus can cause diarrhea, which is often the case if the dog is also running a fever and vomiting. Parasites, in particular tapeworms and roundworms, may also be to blame.

Vomiting

Vomiting may also indicate a bad reaction to an intentional change in diet or a case of the puppy "getting into something." Again, this should resolve within 24 hours. If, however, the dog is trying to vomit but producing no material, if there's blood in the vomit or if the dog cannot keep water down, your pet must be treated immediately by a qualified veterinarian.

Dehydration from vomiting occurs even more quickly than in a case if diarrhea and is potentially fatal. It is possible that your dog may require intravenous fluids.

When your dog is vomiting, always have a good look around to identify what, if anything, the dog may have chewed and swallowed. This can be a huge benefit in targeting appropriate treatment.

Other potential culprits in cases of vomiting include: hookworm, roundworm, pancreatitis, diabetes, thyroid disease, kidney disease, liver disease or a physical obstruction causing a blockage.

Bloat

Any dog can suffer from bloat, but some are at higher risk than others. Also known as gastric dilation/volvulus or GDV, bloat cannot be treated with an antibiotic or prevented with a vaccine. If left untreated, the condition can be fatal.

In the most severe cases, the stomach twists partially or completely, causing major circulation problems in all parts of the digestive system. Dogs that do not receive treatment typically suffer a heart attack, but even if surgical intervention is attempted, there is no guarantee of success.

Signs of bloat are often mistaken for indications of excess gas. The dog may salivate and attempt to vomit, pace frantically and whine. Gas reduction products at this stage can be helpful, but if the stomach swells, pressure is placed on surrounding vital organs, and the stomach itself can burst. All cases of bloat should be treated as a serious medical emergency.

Risk Factors

Larger dogs with deep chests and small waists face a greater risk of developing bloat. These include, among others, the Great Dane, Weimaraner, Saint Bernard, Irish Setter and the Standard Poodle.

Eating habits also factor into the equation. Dogs that eat one large meal per day consisting of dry food are in a high-risk category. Feeding three small meals evenly distributed throughout the day lowers the risk and helps to prevent gulping the food, which leads to the ingestion of large amounts of air.

Although dry food is typically recommended for dogs, they should not be allowed to drink large amounts of water after eating. Doing so causes the dry food in the stomach to swell and expand, leading to discomfort and a dilution of the natural digestive juices. Also, limit the amount of play and exercise a dog receives after eating. A leisurely walk will promote digestion, but a vigorous romp can be dangerous.

Stress also contributes to cases of bloat, especially in dogs that are anxious or nervous by nature. Incidents can be triggered by a change in routine, a disturbing confrontation with another dog or moving to a new home.

Dogs between the ages of 4 and 7 are at the most risk of suffering bloat, which typically occurs between 2 a.m. and 6 a.m., roughly 10 hours after the animal has had his dinner.

Prevention

Feed your pet small meals 2-3 times a day, limiting both water intake and exercise after eating. Take up your pet's water at mealtime, and do not offer it to the dog for at least 30 minutes after your pet finishes his meal. Do not allow strenuous activity for at least an hour.

Test your dog's dry food by putting a portion in a bowl with water and allowing the material to expand overnight. If the degree of added bulk seems excessive, consider switching to a premium or organic food.

After consulting with your veterinarian on correct doses, keep an anti-gas medicine on hand to use in the event that your dog is displaying the signs of discomfort that may precede a case of bloat. Products that contain simethicone are typically recommended. Also consider adding a probiotic to your dog's food to lessen the amount of gas in the animal's stomach and to improve overall digestive health.

If a dog experiences bloat once, his risk of going through a future bout are greatly increased. Be prepared and know the location of the nearest emergency vet clinic. Keep copies of your dog's medical records at home for just such occasions.

Allergies

Dogs, like humans, can suffer adverse allergic reactions to foods, airborne particles or materials that touch their skin. Often owners don't know for certain that their pet is suffering from allergies; they just know that something about the animal's behavior suggests discomfort. Common symptoms include chewing or biting of the tail, stomach or hind legs or licking of the paws to combat itching.

In reaction to inhaled substances, the dog will sneeze, cough or experience watering eyes. Ingested substances may lead to vomiting or diarrhea. Dogs can also suffer from rashes or a case of hives. Simply put, your poor Cockapoo can be just as miserable as you are when something with which you come into contact touches off an allergy.

If the reaction occurs in the spring or fall, the likely culprit is seasonal pollen or, in the case of hot weather, fleas.

Gastrointestinal upsets that cannot be attributed to any direct cause may be a result of food additives like beef, corn, wheat, soybeans and dairy products.

As with any suspected allergy, you can try eliminating items or opting for a special diet, but the only real way to determine what is causing your pet such discomfort is allergy testing. While expensive, often costing \$200+ / £120+, this is the only method that will tell you exactly what needs to be altered in the dog's environment or diet to provide consistent relief.

The vet may recommend medication or simply bathing the dog in cool, soothing water. In many cases, special diets are also extremely helpful.

One particular allergic reaction is quite simple to track down. Acne-like rashes on the chin that may appear as blackheads circled by red irritation are almost always a consequence of plastic feeding dishes. Switch to stainless steel, glass or ceramic. Wash the dog's face in clear, cool water to help the irritation resolve, and consider asking the vet for an antibiotic cream to speed the healing process.

General Signs of Illness

In addition to the specific problems listed above, any of the following symptoms could be an indicator of a more serious medical problem. Have your pet evaluated for any of these behaviors. Do not delay out of concern that you will be perceived as alarmist. Most medical problems in dogs can be resolved if they are treated quickly.

Coughing and/or Wheezing

Occasional coughing is not a cause for concern, but if it goes on for more than a week, a vet visit is in order. A cough may indicate kennel cough, heartworm, cardiac disease, bacterial infections, parasites, tumors or allergies.

Kennel cough is a dry, hacking sound that may follow a period of boarding. Warm, overcrowded conditions with poor airflow cause this upper respiratory condition that is essentially bronchitis. Typically kennel cough resolves spontaneously, but a consultation with the vet is still important. The doctor may prescribe a cough suppressant or suggest the use of a humidifier to soothe your pet's irritated airways.

When the cause of a cough is unclear, the vet will take a full medical history and order tests, including blood work and x-rays. Fluid may also be drawn from the lungs for analysis. Among other conditions, the doctor will be attempting to rule out heartworms.

Photo Credit: Christy Shanklin of Christy's Cockapoos

A Note on Heartworms

Heartworms (*Dirofilaria Immitis*) are transmitted by a mosquito bite. They are thin, long parasites that infest the muscles of the heart, where they block blood vessels and cause bleeding. Their presence can lead to heart failure and death. Coughing and fainting, as well as an intolerance to exercise are all symptoms of heartworm. Discuss heartworm prevention with your vet and decide on the best course of action to keep your pet safe.

Other Warning Signs

In addition to these warning signs discussed above, also be on the lookout for:

- excessive and unexplained drooling
- excessive consumption of water and increased urination
- changes in appetite leading to weight gain or loss
- marked change in levels of activity
- disinterest in favorite activities
- stiffness and difficulty standing or climbing stairs
- sleeping more than normal
- shaking of the head
- any sores, lumps or growths
- dry, red or cloudy eyes

Often the signs of serious illness are subtle. Trust your instincts. If you think something is wrong, do not hesitate to consult with your vet.

Diabetes

Canines can suffer from three types of diabetes: insipidus, diabetes mellitus and gestational diabetes. All point to malfunctioning endocrine glands and are often linked to poor diet, and larger dogs are in a higher risk category.

- Diabetes insipidus occurs when a dog lacks the hormone vasopressin that assists with the regulation of blood glucose and salt as well as water in the body.

- Diabetes mellitus is more common and dangerous. It is broken into Types I and II. The first develops in young dogs and may be referred to as "juvenile." Type II is more prevalent in adult and older dogs. All cases are treated with insulin.

- Gestational diabetes occurs in pregnant female dogs and requires the same treatment as diabetes mellitus. Obese dogs are at greater risk.

When the pancreas no longer produces correct insulin levels in response to food consumption, blood sugar is not processed correctly. Poodles are in the diabetes high-risk group, a prevalence that can be passed into Cockapoos, although in general these crossbred dogs have shown more resistance to the condition.

Symptoms of Canine Diabetes

All of the following behaviors are signs that a dog is suffering from canine diabetes:

- excessive water consumption
- excessive and frequent urination
- lethargy / uncharacteristic laziness
- weight gain or loss for no reason

It is possible, however, that your pet may display no symptoms whatsoever. If the condition comes on slowly, its effects may not be immediately noticeable. Regular check-ups at the vet's help to catch this potentially fatal disease.

Managing Diabetes

As part of an overall program of managing your diabetic dog's condition, the vet will likely recommend dietary changes, including the use of special food. You may also be required to give your pet insulin injections.

Although this may sound daunting, your vet will train you to administer the shots quickly and painlessly. With proper management, a dog with diabetes can live a full and normal life, but must be regularly monitored by your vet, since both heart and circulatory problems can be a consequence of this disease.

Dental Care

Because chewing is a dog's only means of maintaining his teeth, many of our canine friends develop dental problems early in life. Thankfully, dogs are not all that prone to cavities, but they do suffer from accumulations of plaque and associated gum diseases. Often severe halitosis, which is very bad breath, is the first indication that something is wrong.

Typically gingivitis develops first and, if unaddressed, will progress to periodontitis. Warning signs of gum disease may be a reluctance to finish meals, extreme bad breath, swollen and bleeding gums, irregular gum line, plaque build-up, drooling and/or loose teeth. The smaller Poodle varieties are prone to gingivitis, which place Cockapoos at a higher risk as well.

Periodontitis or periodontal disease is a bacterial infection of the gums leading to inflammation and gum recession and possible tooth loss. It requires treatment with antibiotics to prevent a spread of the infection to other parts of the body. Symptoms include puss at the gum line, loss of appetite, depression and irritability, pawing at the mouth, trouble chewing, loose or missing teeth and gastrointestinal upset. Treatment begins with a professional cleaning that may involve root work, descaling and even extractions.

In instances of proliferating gum disease, the gums grow over the teeth causing inflammation and infection. Other symptoms include thickening and lengthening of the gums, bleeding, bad breath, drooling and loss of appetite. Antibiotics are initially prescribed, and surgery is usually required.

Home Dental Care

There are many products available to help with home dental care for your Cockapoo. Some owners opt for water additives that break up tarter and plaque, but in some cases dogs experience stomach upset. Dental sprays and wipes are also an option, but so is gentle gum massage to help break up plaque and tarter.

Most owners incorporate some type of dental chew in their standard care practices. Greenies Dental Chews for Dogs are extremely popular and generally well tolerated in a digestive sense. An added plus is that dogs usually really love them. The treats come in different sizes and are priced in a range of $7 / £4.21 for 22 "Teeny Greenies" and $25 / £15 for 17 Large Greenies.

Actually brushing your pet's teeth is the ultimate defense for overall oral health. This involves the use of both a canine-specific toothbrush and toothpaste. Never use human toothpaste, which contains fluoride toxic to your dog. Some dog toothbrushes resemble smaller versions of our own, but I like the models that just fit over your fingertip. I think they offer far greater control and are more stable than another standard tactic, wrapping gauze around your finger.

The real trick to brushing your pet's teeth is simply getting the dog comfortable with having your hands in his mouth. Start by just massaging the dog's face, and then progressing to the gums before actually using the toothbrush. In the beginning, you can even just smear the toothpaste on the teeth with your fingertip.

Try to schedule these brushing sessions for when the dog is a little tired, perhaps after a long walk. Don't apply pressure, which can stress the dog. Just move in small circular motions and stop when the Cockapoo has had enough of the whole business. If you don't feel you've done enough, a second session is better than forcing your dog to do something he doesn't like and creating a negative association in his mind.

Even if you do practice a full home dental care routine, don't scrimp on annual oral exams in the vet's office. They are very important not only to keep the teeth and gums healthy, but also to check the oral cavity for any growths or lesions that could indicate cancer.

The Matter of Genetic Abnormalities

In the following sections on skeletal health and canine eye care, I will mention conditions that have been associated as genetic abnormalities with Cockapoos. These include progressive retinal atrophy, glaucoma, retinal dysplasia and hip dysplasia.

This, like all topics associated with crossbreeding, is very complicated. For instance, the American Cocker Spaniel shows instances of retinal dysplasia, but the English Cocker Spaniel does not, and the condition is also not frequently associated with Poodles.

The safest and most accurate statement that can be made is that there are known genetic diseases within the gene pool that may affect Cockapoos, and not all are necessarily apparent in puppies. For this reason, you are well advised to ask about health testing of the *parents* used to create the cross.

Health testing will be one of the benchmarks of standardized Cockapoo breeding as the dogs move toward full acceptance as a breed in their own right. If you are dealing with a casual breeder, there will, in all likelihood, have been no advanced health screenings, but a kennel owner with an organized breeding program should be able to discuss this topic with you at length.

Beware of any dog breeder who says health screenings of mated pairs are not necessary or who says no dog in his facility has ever suffered from a genetic condition.

Luxating Patella

A dog with a luxating patella experiences frequent dislocations of the kneecap. The condition is fairly common in small and miniature breeds and can affect one or both kneecaps. Surgery may be required to rectify the problem. Often owners have no idea anything is wrong with their dog's knee join until the pet jumps off a bed or leaps to catch a toy, lands wrong and begins to limp and favor the leg.

The condition may be genetic in origin, so it is important to ask a breeder if the problem has surfaced in the line of dogs he cultivates. A luxating patella can also be the consequence of a physical injury, especially as a dog ages. For this reason, you may want to discourage jumping in older dogs, offering steps in key locations around the home to help your senior Cockapoo navigate more safely.

Any time you see your dog limping or seeming overly fatigued after vigorous play, have the dog checked out. Conditions like a luxating patella only get worse with time and wear and should be treated as soon as possible.

Hip Dysplasia

Cockapoos may also be susceptible to hip dysplasia, a defect that prevents the thighbone from correctly fitting into the hip joint. It is a painful condition that causes limping in the hindquarters. Again, this may be inherited, or the consequence of injury and aging.

When hip dysplasia initially presents itself, the standard treatment is anti-inflammatory medication, but in some cases surgery and even a full hip replacement could be required. The good news is that surgical intervention for this defect is highly successful, allowing your dog to live a full and happy life.

Canine Arthritis

Dogs, like humans, can suffer from arthritis, a debilitating degeneration of the joints seen frequently in larger breeds. As the cartilage in the joints breaks down, the action of bone rubbing on bone creates considerable pain and restricts the animal's range of motion.

Standard treatments for arthritic dogs do not differ all that greatly from those used for humans, including aspirin for pain and inflammation and joint health supplements like glucosamine. Environmental aids, such as steps and ramps, will also ease the strain on the affected joints and help your pet to remain active and engaged in life.

Since arthritis is a natural consequence of aging, management focuses on making your pet comfortable and facilitating ease of motion with assistive devices. Some dogs become so crippled that their humans purchase mobility carts for them. These devices, which attach to the hips, put your pooch on wheels. Cockapoos adapt amazingly well under such circumstances, and so long as your pet is otherwise healthy, this is a reasonable approach to a debilitating but not fatal ailment.

Often called "dog wheelchairs," these units can be purchased online from sites like www.handicappedpets.com, www.k9carts.com and eddieswheels.com. Please note that although the carts are fully adjustable, instances where your dog can be custom fitted for such an appliance may return the greatest mobility and satisfaction.

Canine Eye Care

Dogs eyes are sensitive and should be monitored to avoid problems like clogged tear ducts. Also, many dogs suffer from excessive tearing, which can stain the fur around the eyes and down the muzzle. This is a problem with both Cocker Spaniels and Poodles. As a regular part of good grooming, the corners of your pet's eyes should be kept free of mucus, and the muzzle region should be kept clean to prevent an accumulation of bacteria in the region.

If your dog is prone to mucus accumulation, which is often associated with environmental allergies, ask your vet to recommend a sterile eyewash or gauze pad to clean the eyes safely. Also take the precaution of keeping the hair well trimmed around your pet's eyes. If you do not feel comfortable doing this chore yourself, discuss the problem with your groomer. Shorter hair around the eyes will prevent the transference of bacteria and avoid cases of eye trauma and irritation from scrapes and scratches.

Dogs absolutely love to hang their heads out of car windows, but this can easily result in eye injuries and serious infection from blowing debris. If you don't want to deprive your dog of this simple pleasure, I highly recommend a product called Doggles, which are protective goggles for dogs that come in a range of colors and sizes and are priced at less than $20 / £12 per pair. The investment in protecting your dog's eyes is well worth it, and all of my pets have worn the Doggles without complaint.

Conjunctivitis is the most common eye infection seen in dogs. It presents with redness around the eyes and a green or yellow discharge. The standard treatment is a course of antibiotics and the dreaded "cone of shame" collar, which will keep your pet from scratching and causing greater injury.

Photo Credit: Sylvia Hook of Sylml Cockapoo

Cataracts

Aging dogs often develop cataracts, which is a clouding of the lens of the eye leading to blurred vision. The lesion can vary in size and will be readily apparent as a blue-gray area. In the vast majority of cases, cataracts are monitored but not treated, and typically they do not severely affect your pet's life.

Cherry Eye

The condition commonly called "cherry eye" is an irritation of the third eyelid that appears as a bright pink protrusion in the corner of the eye. It can be caused by an injury or by a bacterial infection. It may occur in one or both eyes and requires surgery to effect a permanent cure.

Glaucoma

Glaucoma is characterized by increased pressure in the eye that prevents proper drainage of fluid. It may develop as a complication when a cataract loosens and shifts, or the condition may develop spontaneously. Dogs with glaucoma typically experience partial or total loss of vision within one year of diagnosis.

Symptoms include swelling, excessive tearing, redness and evident visual limitations. Suspected glaucoma requires immediate medical attention.

PRA or Progressive Retinal Atrophy

The degenerative hereditary disease PRA (progressive retinal atrophy) robs a dog of its vision over time, but progresses slowly, allowing the animal to adapt. There is no way to prevent or cure PRA, and the affected dog will go completely blind. Early detection allows for better environmental adaptations. If you suspected that your Cockapoo's peripheral vision is not good, or if the dog is acting tentative in dark or low light conditions, have your pet's eyes checked.

Among the Cockapoo Club of Great Britain's minimum health test requirements is that one parent is prcd-PRA DNA clear, which will mean that none of the resulting puppies are affected.

Hemorrhagic Gastroenteritis

Any dog can develop hemorrhagic gastroenteritis (HGE), a

potentially fatal condition with a high mortality rate.

Unfortunately, most dog owners have never heard of HGE and do not realize that it must be treated immediately if the dog stands any chance of recovering.

Symptoms include:

- profuse vomiting
- depression
- bloody diarrhea with a foul odor
- severe low blood volume resulting in fatal shock within 24 hours

The exact cause of HGE is unknown, and it often occurs in otherwise healthy dogs. The average age of onset is 2-4 years. Approximately 15% of dogs that survive an attack will suffer a relapse. Miniature Poodles, Miniature Schnauzers, Yorkshire Terriers and Dachshunds all exhibit a higher incidence of HGE than other breeds, but there is no definitive list of high-risk breeds.

The instant your dog vomits or passes blood, get your dog to the vet. Tests will be performed to rule out viral or bacterial infections, ulcers, parasites, cancer and poisoning. X-rays and an electrocardiogram are also primary diagnostic tools for HGE.

Hospitalization and aggressive treatment are necessary. The dog will likely require IV fluids and potentially a blood transfusion. Both steroids and antibiotics are used to prevent infection. If the dog survives, a bland diet is recommended for a week or more with only a gradual reintroduction of normal foods. In almost all cases, the animal will be placed on a special diet for life with the use of a probiotic.

The acute phases of HGE typically lasts 2-3 days. With quick and aggressive treatment, many dogs recover well, but if intervention is delayed for any reason, the outlook is not good.

Photo Credit: Helen Downing of Family Love Kennels

Tail Docking or Cropping

Neither the Cocker Spaniel nor Poodle breeds are dogs born with short tails, but in many cases their tails are docked (shortened) before they are grown. This has raised the controversial subject of docking the tails of Cockapoo puppies.

The vast majority of owners prefer that their dogs not suffer this mutilation, for which there is no justifiable reason beyond perceived aesthetics. Often, however, the procedure has been performed long before prospective adoptive "parents" ever see the puppies.

Some breeders take puppies to the veterinarian, where the dog is anesthetized and the tail surgically shortened. In other cases, however, the breeder removes the tail within five days of birth. This approach assumes that at so young an age, the puppy's nervous system is not yet fully developed and therefore the animal does not feel intense pain.

Two methods are used: cutting off the circulation at the tip of the tail with a strong band until dry gangrene causes it to fall off, or clamping the tail and removing the remaining length with a scalpel or surgical scissors. Regardless of whether the removal is done in a clinic or at home, stitches are required.

If you are against the procedure of docking a dog's tail, state this fact when you contact a breeder about purchasing a Cockapoo. Such a request does likely lock you into taking the dog, but most breeders are willing to leave the tail intact.

The practice is illegal in the United Kingdom and Australia, and there have been efforts in several parts of the United States to impose a similar ban, although no such laws are currently in place.

Rebecca Goins from MoonShine Babies Cockapoo's says this on the subject: "There is also the cut and cauterization technique, which does not require stitches and heals completely within a week to 10 days and many vets and breeders in the US use this technique. I allow new pup parents/owners to request a natural tail, but they have to reserve that pup prior to the procedure. I personally dock my tails to prevent Happy Tail Syndrome.

This is when a very happy dog such as a Cockapoo wags its tail and bangs it against walls, furniture, crate walls and so on to the extent that the tail starts to bleed. Once this happens, you are faced with weeks, months, years of pain and infection and bandaging that will not stay put because of that happy wagging tail. Some vets and owners have tried to bandage the tail to the leg but we all know our Cockapoos will chew this and cause further damage and the sad end to happy tail syndrome is amputation, which is also painful as an adult. Dew claws are also removed because a Cockapoo is a companion and there is no need of dew claws that can cause injury if caught in carpeting, collars, fencing or the eyes on another playful friend. In my 20-plus years of being a Pet Care Tech and Companion Animal Hygienist levels I, II, III (Groomer), I have seen many horrific injuries from dew claws and natural tails left on companion pets such as the Cockapoo."

Breeding Cockapoos

Although there is really nothing to prevent a Cockapoo owner from breeding their dog, the results may be unpredictable depending on the other dog used in the pairing. If a Cockapoo is bred back to a Cocker Spaniel, the puppies will be more spaniel-like; to a Poodle, more poodle-like.

This may not be a problem for casual pairings, but for breeders truly interested in furthering Cockapoos as a distinct breed in their own right, a more detailed genetic understanding is necessary.

F1 Cockapoo bred to another F1 Cockapoo will result in a whole litter of puppies with a charming Cockapoo nature, but in that same litter, they may inherit any one of four different coat types:

- A flat coat like a Cocker Spaniel that will probably shed but therefore be low maintenance for grooming.

- A straight coat that will ultimately develop loose waves in a coat that will grow to 4"-5" long if left that may be very low shedding and need a medium/high degree of grooming and generally will be trimmed into a teddy bear trim of up to 2" long to be practical on a daily basis.

- A ringlet/wavy coat that is typical of a puppy that looks like a teddy bear at 8 weeks old, this coat will grow long and thick into a full ringlet and probably will not shed, which will make grooming out the undercoat difficult. A high maintenance coat that is best trimmed every 6 weeks into a teddy bear trim of 1" - 2" long.

- A Poodle coat – a tight curl that is high maintenance and needs regular trimming into a teddy bear trim.

The Genetics of Generations

The first (F1) generation cross, created by mating a Cocker Spaniel and a Poodle, is the most stable in terms of health and longevity. These dogs will show the greatest degree of visual difference from the parents.

In an F2 crossing, both parents are F1 Cockapoos. The result of such a pairing can revert due to the "Granddad Effect," so that the puppies look more like one of the original purebred grandparents.

An F3 Cockapoo has two F2 parents, and an F4 has two F3 parents. These are the pairings that will begin to show more generalized traits as the breed works toward greater stabilization.

If at any time a Cockapoo is bred back to one of the core breeds (Cocker Spaniel or Poodle) a "b" is added to the variation description. If, for instance, an F1 Cockapoo was bred back to a Poodle to get a tighter coat, the puppies would be described as F1b.

Why Breed?

If you are simply the owner of a great dog and you want to raise a litter of puppies, that may be reason enough, but if you are someone truly interested in seeing the Cockapoo recognized as an independent breed, this project may be an all-consuming passion.

None of the old wives tales about a female dog being healthier for having given birth to a litter before being spayed are true. For real Cockapoo enthusiasts, the only reason to breed their dogs is to improve the genetics of the line.

Photo Credit: Rebecca Goins of MoonShine Babies Cockapoos

In the true tradition of the dog fancy, these people will carefully select mated pairs for the likely results in the litter. Meticulous records of the mating will be kept to build an ancestral bloodline from which subsequent generations of Cockapoos will be bred.

Some groups, like the Cockapoo Club of Great Britain, are working to establish a registry for Cockapoos to enhance the development of the Cockapoo breed and to make DNA testing a standard in selecting mated pairs.

Chapter 8 – Preparing for Older Age

It can be heartbreaking to watch your beloved pet grow older – he may develop health problems like arthritis, and he simply might not be as active as he once was.

Unfortunately, aging is a natural part of life that cannot be avoided. All you can do is learn how to provide for your Cockapoo's needs as he ages so you can keep him with you for as long as possible.

Photo Credit: Stephen Charlton of Jukee Doodles

What to Expect

Aging is a natural part of life for both humans and dogs. Sadly, dogs reach the end of their lives sooner than most humans do.

Once your Cockapoo reaches the age of 8 years or so, he can be considered a "senior" dog.

At this point, you may need to start feeding him a dog food specially formulated for older dogs, and you may need to take some other precautions as well.

In order to properly care for your Cockapoo as he ages, you might find it helpful to know what to expect. On this page, you will find a list of things to expect as your Cockapoo dog starts to get older:

- Your dog may be less active than he was in his youth – he will likely still enjoy walks, but he may not last as long as he once did and he might take it at a slower pace.

- Your Cockapoo's joints may start to give him trouble – check for signs of swelling and stiffness and consult your veterinarian with any problems.

- Your dog may sleep more than he once did – this is natural sign of aging but it can also be a symptom of a health problem, so consult your vet if your dog's sleeping becomes excessive.

- Your dog may have a greater tendency to gain weight, so you will need to carefully monitor his diet to keep him from becoming obese in his old age.

- Your dog may have trouble walking or jumping so keep

an eye on your Cockapoo if he has difficulty jumping, or if he starts dragging his back feet.

- Your dog's vision may no longer be as sharp as it once was so your Cockapoo may be predisposed to these problems.

- You may need to trim your Cockapoo's nails more frequently if he doesn't spend as much time outside as he once did when he was younger.

- Your dog may be more sensitive to extreme heat and cold, so make sure he has a comfortable place to lie down both inside and outside.

- Your dog will develop gray hair around the face and muzzle – this may be less noticeable in Cockapoos with a lighter coat.

While many of the signs mentioned above are natural side effects of aging, they can also be symptoms of serious health conditions. If your dog develops any of these problems suddenly, consult your veterinarian immediately.

Caring for an Older Cockapoo

When your Cockapoo gets older, he may require different care than he did when he was younger.

The more you know about what to expect as your Cockapoo ages, the better equipped you will be to provide him with the care he needs to remain healthy and mobile.

Here are some tips for caring for your Cockapoo dog as he ages:

- Schedule routine annual visits with your veterinarian to make sure your Cockapoo is in good condition.

- Consider switching to a dog food that is specially formulated for senior dogs – a food that is too high in calories may cause your dog to gain weight.

- Supplement your dog's diet with DHA and EPA fatty acids to help prevent joint stiffness and arthritis.

- Brush your Cockapoo's teeth regularly to prevent periodontal diseases, which are fairly common in older dogs.

- Continue to exercise your dog on a regular basis – he may not be able to move as quickly, but you still need to keep him active to maintain joint and muscle health.

- Provide your Cockapoo with soft bedding on which to sleep – the hard floor may aggravate his joints and worsen arthritis.

- Use ramps to get your dog into the car and onto the bed, if he is allowed, because he may no longer be able to jump.

- Consider putting down carpet or rugs on hard floors – slippery hardwood or tile flooring can be very problematic for arthritic dogs.

In addition to taking some of the precautions listed above in caring for your elderly Cockapoo, you may want to familiarize yourself with some of the health conditions your dog is likely to develop in his old age.

Elderly dogs are also likely to exhibit certain changes in behavior, including:

- Confusion or disorientation
- Increased irritability
- Decreased responsiveness to commands
- Increase in vocalization (barking, whining, etc.)
- Heightened reaction to sound
- Increased aggression or protectiveness
- Changes in sleep habits
- Increase in house soiling accidents

As he ages, these tendencies may increase – he may also become more protective of you around strangers.

As your Cockapoo gets older, you may find that he responds to your commands even less frequently than he used to.

The most important thing you can do for your senior dog is to schedule regular visits with your veterinarian. You should also, however, keep an eye out for signs of disease as your dog ages.

The following are common signs of disease in elderly dogs:

- Decreased appetite
- Increased thirst and urination
- Difficulty urinating/constipation
- Blood in the urine
- Difficulty breathing/coughing
- Vomiting or diarrhea
- Poor coat condition

If you notice your elderly Cockapoo exhibiting any of these symptoms, you would be wise to seek veterinary care for your dog as soon as possible.

Euthanasia

The hardest decision any pet owner makes is helping a suffering animal to pass easily and humanely. I have been in this position, and even though I know my beloved companied died peacefully and with no pain, my own anguish was considerable. Thankfully, I was in the care of and accepting the advice and counsel of exceptional veterinary professionals.

This is the crucial component in the decision to euthanize an animal. For your own peace of mind, you must know that you have been given the best medical advice possible. My vet was not only knowledgeable and patient, but she was kind and forthright. I valued all of those qualities and hope you are as blessed as I was in the same situation.

But the bottom line is this. No one is in a position to judge you. *No one.* You must make the best decision that you can for your pet and for yourself. So long as you are acting from a position of love, respect and responsibility, whatever you do is "right."

Grieving a Lost Pet

Some humans have difficulty fully recognizing the terrible grief involved in losing a beloved canine friend.

There will be many who do not understand the close bond we humans can have with our dogs, which is often unlike any we have with our human counterparts.

Your friends may give you pitying looks and try to cheer you up, but if they have never experienced the loss of such a special connection themselves, they may also secretly think you are making too much fuss over "just a dog."

For some of us humans, the loss of a beloved dog is so painful that we decide never to share our lives with another, because the thought of going through the pain of such a loss is unbearable. Expect to feel terribly sad, tearful and yes, depressed, because those who are close to their canine companions will feel their loss no less acutely than the loss of a human friend or life partner.

The grieving process can take some time to recover from, and some of us never totally recover.

After the loss of a family dog, first you need to take care of yourself by making certain that you remember to eat regular meals and get enough sleep, even though you will feel an almost eerie sense of loneliness.

Losing a beloved dog is a shock to the system that can also affect your concentration and your ability to find joy or be interested in participating in other activities that are a normal part of your daily life.

Other dogs, cats and pets in the home will also be grieving the loss of a companion and may display this by acting depressed, being off their food or showing little interest in play or games.

Therefore, you need to help guide your other pets through this grieving process by keeping them busy and interested, taking them for extra walks and finding ways to spend more time with them.

Wait Long Enough

Many people do not wait long enough before attempting to replace a lost pet and will immediately go to the local shelter and rescue a deserving dog. While this may help to distract you from your grieving process, this is not really fair to the new fur member of your family.

Bringing a new pet into a home that is depressed and grieving the loss of a long-time canine member may create behavioral problems for the new dog that will be faced with learning all about their new home, while also dealing with the unstable energy of the grieving family.

A better scenario would be to allow yourself the time to properly grieve by waiting a minimum of one month to allow yourself and your family to feel happier and more stable before deciding upon sharing your home with another dog.

Photo Credit: Malinda DeVincenzi of Darby Park Doodles

Managing Health Care Costs

Thanks to advances in veterinary science, there are now more viable and effective treatments available for our pets. The estimated annual cost for maintaining a medium-sized dog, including health care, is approximately $650 / £387. (This does not, of course, include figures for emergency care, advanced procedures, or consultations with specialists.)

Many vets have created clubs where members pay $15 / $20 (£10 / £15) a month – you get discounts on all bills and vaccinations each year, plus worm and flea treatment and check-ups.

The growing interest in pet insurance to help defray these costs is perfectly understandable. It may be possible to purchase comprehensive pet insurance, including coverage for accidents, illness and even some hereditary and chronic conditions, for as little as $25 / £16.25 per month. Benefit caps and deductibles vary by company.

To obtain rate quotes, investigate the following companies in the United States and the UK:

United States

http://www.24PetWatch.com
http://www.ASPCAPetInsurance.com
http://www.EmbracePetInsurance.com
http://www.HealthyPawsPetInsurance.com
http://www.PetsBest.com
http://www.PetInsurance.com

United Kingdom

http://www.Animalfriends.org.uk
http://www.Healthy-pets.co.uk
http://www.Petplan.co.uk
http://www.Vetsmedicover.co.uk

Afterword

When "designer dogs" first begin to be the "in" thing, I have to confess I looked askance at the entire phenomenon. I'm especially against breeding crosses that create exaggerated physical traits that have a dramatic effect on how the dog will be able to live in the world.

As you can clearly see, there are no such unrealistic goals behind the cultivation of the Cockapoo breed. The foundation dogs are both highly regarded companion animals with the ethos of working dogs. They both have a reputation for excellent dispositions and for robust health.

When those qualities emerge in the Cockapoo, the result is nothing short of remarkable. The personality of a Cockapoo swells to delightfully epic proportions. They are dogs consumed with energy, fun and a zest for life. Up for any adventure, endlessly good humored to the point of being comical and utterly devoted to their humans, this dog will indeed be your best friend.

At the same time, Cockapoos are terrifically empathetic, sensing and really understanding your moods and trying to "fix" things for you. They excel in therapy dog work and are a great comfort and joy for elderly owners. A Cockapoo is also a perfect dog for a child. They're just that affable and that flexible.

Several times in the text, I've described Cockapoos as a breed in transition. They are not yet formally recognized by any governing body in the dog fancy as an official breed per se, but I have no doubt that will happen. The widespread popularity of the cross, both in the United States and in the UK, is generating more and more serious breeding programs.

Enthusiasts are working assiduously to refine the qualities of the Cockapoo line, and the popularity of the animals is easily spread by the efforts of the dogs themselves. To meet a Cockapoo for the first time is to fall in love.

So long as you can meet the dog's physical and emotional needs and cater to its true requirement for companionship, the Cockapoo is a near perfect companion. Just be prepared to answer one question over and over again, "What kind of dog is *that*?"

That is a Cockapoo, and there's no other dog quite like him.

Photo Credit: Stephen Charlton of Jukee Doodles

Bonus Chapter 1 - The Cockapoo Club of Great Britain

The information in this chapter has been provided by the Cockapoo Club of Great Britain for the benefit of our British readers.

With a history of 25 years of breeding Champion Trakehner horses in a farming environment, Julia Charlton worked Border Collies with sheep, and there was a family Springer Spaniel that worked to the gun.

In the search for a house dog for their 3-year-old daughter, Julia went to view one of the first Cockapoo breeders in UK, an International Grooming competitor and judge, who had come across Cockapoos at shows in USA and had been so taken with the dogs that they brought the concept home and began breeding their Miniature Poodles with English Show Cocker Spaniels.

Already with an experienced eye for breeding, Julia felt that though they were very cute, fluffy and healthy, they didn't match up to what she wanted from a pet. Wanting the intense eye contact and willingness to please that she'd enjoyed with working dogs, she decided to breed from English Working Cocker Spaniel bitches and a Miniature Poodle dad. From the first litter of Cockapoo puppies that she advertised on the Internet, which resulted in 50 enquiries, the level of interest hasn't stopped to this day.

Stephen and Julia met and married in 2008 when Julia had four pet English Working Cocker Spaniel bitches and a Miniature Poodle stud dog and was classed as a hobby breeder. Over the last few years, not only has demand for their Cockapoo puppies soared but Stephen, not previously a "doggy" man, has found his calling, loves the outdoor lifestyle working with the dogs and Jukee Doodles was born.

Jukee Doodles, now a thriving business, runs up to 16 Working Cocker Spaniel breeding bitches and three Miniature Poodle stud dogs, only breeding Cockapoos and loving what they do.

After a few years of breeding and seeing the increase of unregulated breeding and unethical practices being reported by Cockapoo buyers, Stephen became active in the network of people and organisations that were trying to raise awareness in the UK. He worked on the Cockapoo pages for Carole Fowler's website "Dog Breed Health," worked on Channel 4's Dispatches programme and the "Farms of Shame" site to help expose the darker side of dog breeding in the UK. Along with being Breed Advisor for "Dogs Today" magazine, he was invited to represent the Cockapoo at the 2014 National Pet Show at the National Exhibition Centre in the Discover Dogs Section.

Seeing the need to "protect the Cockapoo of tomorrow, today," Stephen conceived the idea of having a website to raise awareness and give information to those wishing to research the Cockapoo dog. He approached more than twenty people who had expressed strong and balanced opinions online, and very quickly a team of 17 founding members set to work, all writing, debating and editing what has become The Cockapoo Club of GB (CCGB) in November 2011. Since that launch, the CCGB has rapidly evolved and in under three years already boasts an international membership, as the popularity of the Cockapoo is spreading into Europe and beyond.

The Cockapoo Club of Great Britain was formed by a group of owners, breeders and enthusiasts who wish to promote the health and welfare of the increasingly growing number of Cockapoos being bred in Great Britain in recent years.

With their cute appearance and sweet, biddable, cheeky and loving characters, there is an ever-increasing number of breeders getting involved. Their objective is to inform and educate as to the best way to produce, care for and have fun with this appealing cross-breed.

Approved Breeder Scheme

As the population increases and in time more Cockapoos are bred to other Cockapoos, they aim to keep adding to their in-house database of parentage, together with the relevant health tests, by means of registration.

This will allow breeders to make educated decisions on which pairings will produce puppies with good character and free from hereditary disease, deformity and in-breeding, and will provide buyers with invaluable information when researching which puppy / dog to purchase.

As the Cockapoo is considered an ideal family pet, assistance dog, working dog or activity sport dog and is not destined for the show ring, the emphasis is on promoting a Breeding Standard as opposed to a Breed Standard.

The CCGB place importance on function over form. The varied appearance of Cockapoos are all acceptable using breeding stock from the core breeds of the American Show Cocker Spaniels,

English Show Cocker Spaniels and English Working Cocker Spaniels mixed with either Toy Poodles or Miniature Poodles.

Whilst breeding with the Teacup or the Standard Poodle does happen, it is not encouraged nor can they be registered, as it is considered to be outside the recommended size to physically breed with cocker spaniels.

To this end, the CCGB Inspectors visit each breeder applicant, check health test records, inspect breeders' premises and animals and advise of the CCGB Code of Ethics, animal welfare and further health testing.

They offer the ongoing support of the CCGB by way of the breeder being able to network directly with other Approved Breeder Members, and the Inspectors advise on how best to offer lifelong support to puppy buyers, including how to raise, care for and train their dogs into adulthood through the medium of the Cockapoo Club Chat Forum.

The CCGB Inspectors play an essential part in the assessment process and report their findings to the CCGB Registrar and the

Committee as a whole for further consideration.

Once approved, a breeder will be listed on the CCGB website, and they will be eligible to apply for official CCGB lineage papers for the Cockapoo puppies that they breed.

CCGB Rescue, Rehoming and Respite

Thankfully, it is still relatively uncommon for a Cockapoo to be offered for rehoming, as most puppies are wanted and find their forever home and family immediately. However, there are some circumstances that arise which make it necessary to re-home a Cockapoo.

There are many reasons why buying a puppy for a particular person may not have the positive outcome that most people experience.

Sadly, some people get a puppy without realising how much time and effort they require and so then re-sell the puppy. This is often why most of the dogs found on the Internet that are advertised for sale (not by breeders) are between 9 and 20 weeks old.

Ordinarily, your breeder should be your first point of contact should rehoming be needed. All reputable breeders will offer a lifetime of help and support for a dog they have bred and should ask that the dog be returned to them should any problems arise at any point.

Sometimes, however, this is not possible, and rather than re-selling or giving away a Cockapoo, owners contact the CCGB RRR, who have an excellent record of being able to help and re-home the dog, as they have a large database with many members who register an interest in offering a stable, permanent home to a

Cockapoo in need.

It can be very difficult and stressful, so they help people that have sadly come to this decision by offering an empathic ear where the situation can be discussed freely without judgement.

Offering a supportive service tailor made to each given situation, whether that be giving respite care in a temporary foster home through to finding a new forever home, assessments and interviews are carried out and a register kept of any dog re-homed to ensure that each Cockapoo has been placed in the very best home.

Respite care can be offered where the CCGB or one of their registered foster carers takes the Cockapoo into their home to stay for a pre-arranged period of time in situations where personal circumstances change, which make looking after the Cockapoo difficult until some permanent rearrangements to a lifestyle can be made. The intention is then that the Cockapoo will return home when the environment is suitable again.

Cockapoo Club Chat Forum

Through their Cockapoo Club Chat Forum, thousands of members support Cockapoo owners internationally. Through this medium, many introductions and real friendships have been formed where members regularly arrange group walks, meets and glamping weekends at venues all over the UK and Europe.

The active social calendar culminates at the annual Cockapoo Games held in the Autumn with an international gathering of Cockapoos and their owners. More than doubling each year it has been held, the third Cockapoo Games in August 2014 hosted over 600 visitors and 228 Cockapoo in their "Poo Parade."

Photo Credit: Lisa Tatterson of Furrtography

More information can be found on the CCGB website:
http://www.cockapooclubgb.co.uk

Bonus Chapter 2 - Shannon Wallace Interview

Shannon thanks for doing this interview, can you tell us who you are and where you are based?

I am Shannon Wallace. I have shown dogs for many years in American Kennel Club shows. Mainly Dobermans before I was "bit" by the Cockapoo bug. I have produced a Doberman that made it into the Top 20 in conformation. After doing this for a number of years and having a litter or two of Cockapoos on the side, as it were, I fell completely in love with the breed and decided to concentrate on Cockapoos alone. I am located in the United States from Indiana but also work as a dog groomer in Kentucky.

I know you have been breeding Cockapoos longer than most, can you tell us how long and how did it all start?

The year 2014 marks my 11th year breeding Cockapoos. My mother always had American Cocker Spaniels and I had Dobermans. In 2002 my mother and I purchased and bred a Buff Cocker Spaniel named Keisha. She produced my black and tan Cocker Spaniel named Fluff that later became a matriarch at OZ Cockapoos.

In 2003 we bought Keisha's litter sister named Hannah. I have a friend whose son was allergic to most dogs. He had done well with a Cockapoo so on a lark I bred Hannah with a friend's Toy Poodle in North Carolina. I know I went pretty far for this breeding but this boy was worth it. I did mention I showed dogs in conformation right? Well this Poodle was square, and moved like a dream. Correct bite, great coat and well worth the trip.

My first Cockapoo litter arrived November 16th, 2003. It consisted of three buff males and three buff females. Buff is a golden color. I had one litter in 2004 and by then the bug had caught fire. In 2005 I became involved with other Cockapoo breeders and had my very first merle Cockapoo litter (there weren't many merles around at that time).

What types of people are buying Cockapoos and why?

I have a variety of people buy Cockapoos. Mainly those that have allergies to pet dander or those that just want a loving, intelligent pet. I have had Cockapoos go all over the world. I even have one in France.

The Cockapoo is not recognized by the American Kennel Club, is it a question or issue that is raised by many people?

Cocker Spaniels had a bad reputation back in the 1980s due to the breed becoming very popular and people not researching the Cocker Spaniel breed or bloodlines before making puppies. This happens in EVERY SINGLE BREED. That is where the choice of a breeder is more important than the actual dog. With the right breeder you will find the dog meant for your family.

Most people that are looking for a Cockapoo do not care that it is not AKC registered. AKC registered breeds started out as a purposeful mixture of multiple dogs for a certain purpose which later became a known breed.

What sort of challenges do you face in mating two different breeds?

The greatest challenge as a breeder of the Cockapoo is to find that "perfect" match between the Cocker Spaniel and the Poodle. That is the most difficult thing to do. I want correct conformation in my parent dogs. I want a nice square body, correct bite, full muzzle. I have seen several Cockapoos with short legs and long backs. I would not choose to breed this look.

You also want to have health be a priority. People talk about the hybrid vigor and while this is true to a certain scale it is not completely true. Because this is a cross between the Cocker Spaniel and the Poodle, these breeds have similar health issues. PRA is one of those. That is Progressive Retinal Atrophy (PRA), which is an inherited disease of the retina in dogs, in which the rod cells in the retina are programmed to die. PRA occurs in both eyes simultaneously and is non-painful. PRA occurs in most breeds of dogs and also occurs in mixed breeds.

I feel a Cockapoo should have the agility and stamina to go on long hikes. They should have the calm demeanor to become a therapy dog. They should have the smarts and instinct to become a SAR dog. Should have the patience to deal with a toddler that wants to hold them by the ears. Should have the health to live 15+ years.

What type of health issues can a Cockapoo have and how do you deal with preventing these?

There are health tests to check for patella luxation or hip and elbow problems in your Cockapoo parents. An annual CERF test can let you be aware if any abnormal eye issues are showing up. We have a specialist that can do heart monitoring as well as liver and kidney panels. Thank goodness that there is a DNA test that tells you if your dog is clear, a carrier or affected with PRA. Even with an affected dog, if everything else about the dog should be contributed to the breed, you breed that dog to a clear parent and it will give you 100% carrier pups. This means your puppy will never ever have PRA and if that puppy is also bred to a clear then you will get 50% clear and 50% carrier. So never "throw the baby out with the bathwater" as the old saying goes. Just use what tests we have and try to set your goal on a realistic basis.

We know the Cockapoo can vary depending on a number of factors, what type of Cockapoo is most popular?

A red Cockapoo or one of a golden color seems to be the most desirable in the Cockapoo. They all want the "Teddy Bear" look. I have developed a more consistent look over the years. When I first started out I had a lot of Cockapoos with under bites, coats were all over the place. By concentrating on what I wanted to bring into this breed I have now developed a system where my multi-generation Cockapoos (those with two Cockapoo parents) are looking like my first generation Cockapoos (those with a Cocker Spaniel parent and a Poodle parent).

Is it possible to describe a fairly typical Cockapoo so people know what to expect?

Cockapoos are a wonderful breed. Sometimes they are too intelligent for the owners and the owners become frustrated. I do believe that it is important to have a dog trainer when the puppy comes home in order to teach the owner what to do and what not to do.

Cockapoos want to have their minds worked and want to learn. They are never happier except when learning new and exciting things. A Cockapoo is a "heart dog." Those are the ones that crawl into your heart and soul and you will feel lost without them. Cockapoos have great instinct and if they don't like a person you might want to take a closer look. They are protective of family and home. They are agile and fearless.

Because Cockapoos come from a sporting breed and have such high intelligence, they can develop resource guarding which if handled correctly at a young age goes away easily and is not a problem in the future. Resource guarding is normal and natural in all dogs.

Potty training varies depending on the temperament of the dog and any possible issues like urinary tract infections.

Can you offer advice to people looking to buy a Cockapoo and how much do they cost?

The average cost of a Cockapoo puppy from health-tested parents and a responsible breeder is from $1000-$1900 at this time depending on demographic areas.

Finding the right breeder is the biggest step in getting the right puppy for your family. You want a breeder that will be there for you. You will have a lifetime of good times with your Cockapoo but at the end you want that breeder there to hold your hand even if just in a phone call. I don't know about all breeders but I was there for the first breath, the first cry and the first step. I want to be there, even if only a shoulder to cry on, for the last step and the last breath. When you get a puppy from me we are attached at the hip and I want to hear about all the amazing things your Cockapoo does but also any concerns. There is never a dumb question – ask anyone, I answer even at two in the morning.

As a breed expert, are there any 'essential' tips you would like to share with new owners?

I know a lot of people want to pick the puppy themselves and want that puppy that chooses you. Well a lot of times that puppy that chooses you and climbs up to kiss you on the mouth and bite at your hands is a dominant puppy. If you have children this is not the puppy for your family.

Trust in your breeder to help you pick the right puppy for your family. Talk to your breeder about your activity level and be truthful above all. Research your breeder and talk to others that have puppies from them. Go to your breeder with any questions or concerns in purchasing your puppy.

Get puppy health insurance. Several breeders offer a free 30 days of insurance. Use it, it's free. It can save you thousands. Make sure you look up and study what plants and foods are bad for your puppy. Have poison control for animals written down because you will not believe what your puppy might get into. If you are not ready to deal with a seven-month-old baby crawling around on the floor without a diaper, you are not ready for a puppy.

Thanks so much Shannon for sharing your expertise and for sharing your unique story with everyone.

Shannon Wallace - OZ Cockapoos
http://www.ozcockapoos.net/

Bonus Chapter 3 - Malinda DeVincenzi Interview

Malinda thanks for doing this interview, can you tell us who you are and where you are based?

My name is Malinda DeVincenzi. I'm a mom to my son Brandon, a wife to my husband Terry, and professional breeder of Cockapoos and Australian Labradoodles. I own and operate Darby Park Doodles, a licensed home business in Brentwood, Northern California.

My breeding program is unique in that it is a kennel-free environment for both my breeding dogs and their puppies. My dogs and puppies are raised in a clean and healthy environment within my home, or that of one of my Guardian Families' homes. I proudly share my home with three beautiful furry girls: Molly, Darby and Kimber.

When I'm not tending to family and puppies, you can usually find me volunteering my time to one of the many causes I'm passionate about. My husband and son are avid fishermen, and I'm very supportive of their sport. Alongside volunteering with my son's high school fishing club, I also recently founded and coordinate an afterschool youth fishing program.

When in between litters, one would not know I'm a dog breeder. When my breeding dogs are not active in a breeding period, they live comfortably with their guardian family. Having a "Guardian Home"-based breeding program allows each and every one of the dogs in my breeding program to have a normal happy dog life, from their puppyhood through their senior years. It's important to note, that if not for the families participating in my Guardian Home Program, I would not be able to keep such an active calendar. I hold a lot of appreciation and gratitude towards my guardian families. With so many helping hands, I'm able to properly raise, socialize and keep each and every litter healthy.

How long have you been involved in breeding Cockapoos and what made you get started?

Coming from an animal rescue shelter background, I did not envision my future as a dog breeder. In the mid 1970s, my mom had been working in a veterinary office, and it was there that her compassion towards the countless abandoned pets drove her to opening an animal shelter. This was documented in a 1978 pet magazine – my mom was featured in one of the pictures with a rescued litter of Cockapoo puppies. It was then that we first came to know Cockapoos and their wonderful temperaments.

Over 20 years later, and just a year after my son was born, I brought two non-shedding poodle mix puppies (Cockapoos) from my mom's animal shelter to an early childhood development school for special needs children. It was there I saw the therapeutic qualities of these puppies and the positive imprint they made on the children. With the desire to stay home and raise my son, it was shortly thereafter I resigned from my job at a veterinary hospital to pursue breeding therapy dogs.

The combination of a sweet-natured dog, with a non-shedding and allergy-friendly coat, was the foundation of what I was looking for to start breeding therapy-quality companion dogs.

Today, I breed many Cockapoo bloodlines suitable for therapy work with healthcare professionals. These professionals seek out

Cockapoos to be in their workplace to provide patients with comfort or to help stimulate them in an uplifting, positive way.

Over the past decade, I've worked with a wide range of clients. In my opinion, dogs in general are therapy for people, although many people need something more specific to suit their families' special circumstances. Some clients seek the love and companionship of a Cockapoo because they suffer from post-traumatic stress disorder, depression or maybe they're confined to a wheelchair. I most enjoy working with families that have children with special needs, as it was my driving force behind breeding Cockapoos.

Many of my clients, ones that are passionate about volunteer work, purchase my Cockapoos so they can also train them as certified service dogs. With that, they are able to bring them to hospitals or senior living facilities for meet and greets. Just as I once did before I started breeding.

Given your long history with the Cockapoo, perhaps you could enlighten our readers with some insights into how the breed began, whether it is becoming more popular or less as time goes on, perhaps your thoughts on how you see the breed progressing?

In my opinion, Cockapoos have become a mainstream breed. Documented at least back to the 60s, Cockapoos have grown in popularity, and have become a common household breed. It should be noted that Cockapoos were already a known crossbreed well before the growing popularity of the "poo" cross breeds that started in the 1990s. Cockapoos are truly not a fad breed and will be around for generations.

What can a new owner expect in terms of differences between this breed and others?

Most Cockapoos are bred for low to non-shedding coats, which are great for people who suffer from allergies or asthma. The majority of breeds shed, so Cockapoos are commonly a top choice for people with dog allergies.

Cockapoos are also known to be a child-friendly breed. When properly trained and raised alongside children, this breed becomes a close family member that can be incorporated into a family's everyday routine, inside and outside of the home. Their friendly nature, smaller size and low to non-shedding coats makes it easy to travel with a Cockapoo.

Can you offer advice to people looking to buy a Cockapoo?

Make sure timing is right before adopting a Cockapoo. To start, children should be at least 5 years old prior to adopting a puppy. In addition, it's never a good idea to adopt if all adults in the household work away from the home full time. Also, do not plan any immediate vacations for at least 6 months, as consistency is so important to quickly and properly training your puppy.

Select only well-known breeders with references. Be sure they have done breed appropriate health screenings on the parent dogs. Look for a breeder that is willing to evaluate puppies beyond 6 weeks old so they can better match you with the right temperament for your family.

Always have a trainer picked out prior taking home a puppy. Many people believe you only need a trainer if there's something wrong with your dog. That's simply not the case. Most families need guidance from day one to prevent or detect undesirable puppy behaviors that many pups, of any breed, can have their first year.

Knowing how to handle an undesirable behavior before it

becomes a problem can prevent months of frustration, and help you maintain a positive relationship with your puppy. It can also be costly to reverse behaviors that were allowed to go on far too long. For experienced dog owners, please consider that you are likely to have a different experience with every new dog that comes into your home. It's truly best to be prepared and plan ahead.

In general, Cockapoos are considered a family-friendly breed, but no two pups are created equal. Because of this, it's important to work with a breeder that's willing to evaluate puppies as individuals, from birth to 8 weeks old, so they can properly match the right type of puppy temperament to each new family.

Ongoing temperament evaluations are most important through the ages of 5-8 weeks old, and puppies should not be matched with families prior to the completion of these evaluations at 8 weeks old.

Are there things that you see owners doing that frustrate you?

Yes, at times and one thing is this – when they feel crate training or puppy play pens are too confining for a puppy, so they let the puppy have free roam of too large of an area in their home. Then the common complaint I would hear would is that the puppy is not trainable and potties all over their house.

It's so important to understand that most puppies are a reflection of the owner's own style of training. Experienced professional dog trainers can explain this best, and I'm not a trainer, but one common analogy I've heard from trainers over the years is that you can hypothetically take the same puppy, start it out in 5 different households, and that puppy can turn out 5 completely different ways. Ranging anywhere from being a certified canine good citizen or therapy dog, to a barky aggressive biter that pees all over the house. Understanding what it means to be a responsible dog parent is one of the most important steps to take before adopting a new family member into your home.

What would be the positives and negatives of owning a Cockapoo?

A positive to owning a Cockapoo is that they have low to non-shedding coats, which is great for allergy sufferers. With the lower and non-shedding coats comes a much lower to almost non-existent dog odor, as this mostly comes from their skin and coats. The other added bonus to a non-shedding dog is that it keeps your house clean of dog fur. The downside to the Cockapoo coat is that they do require more grooming. Most often, owners prefer professional grooming so there's an added cost to owning a Cockapoo.

What feeding routines and types of food/supplements do you recommend?

I recommend feeding a dry food diet twice daily. Every brand of food has specific portion recommendations written on the bag. It's based on the type of food and your dog's age and size. Feeding dry food promotes better dental hygiene by the hard kibble scraping against the teeth therefore helping reduce plaque.

I would highly recommend never feeding canned food. It contributes to tooth decay and can also cause softer, smellier stools.

Cockapoos benefit from premium quality foods. Foods with less by-products and more whole meats such as lamb, duck and fish formulas. Grain free is also beneficial, as many Cockapoos have food allergies and are allergic to corn, wheat and even soy. My favorite food to feed is Pinnacle Trout and Sweet Potato Formula.

Also, you should never feed table scraps. Once they get a taste of it, they will beg for it and seek it out. Seeking it out and finding it can be very dangerous for your dog, especially if you're not home.

There are many foods that are toxic to dogs, so be sure to research what these foods are in case your dog ever encounters them.

Having healthy dog treats and dog chews will help your dog feel fulfilled. If your dog is on a special diet, like a grain-free food, be sure to stick to a grain-free treat too. One of the long-time veterinary- and trainer-recommended treats are freeze-dried liver treats.

As for dog chews, be sure to stick with all-natural, 100% digestible rawhide such as Bully Sticks, Pig Ears and Cow Hooves. These will also help keep their teeth clean.

Are there accessories that you can particularly recommend owners buy?

I would highly recommend a wire crate that will fit the size of your dog full grown. Be sure to purchase the one with the divider so you can section off a smaller area for when it's a pup.

A puppy "play pen" or "exercise pen" is also a great tool in house training. This is a place for your puppy to stretch his legs, play with toys or eat its meals when you're not actively available to supervise or interact with your puppy.

Be sure to provide a variety of toys at all times so the puppy has plenty of things to stimulate him.

Also, keep in mind that Cockapoos have thicker and longer coats, so especially if you're bringing home a puppy in the summer, be sure not to have a fitted bed pad in the crate. The puppy will not be able to escape the heat. Instead, use towels or small baby blankets in the beginning weeks until you find what room and temperature is comfortable for your puppy. Covering the crate with a blanket will also help your puppy rest easy.

Another reason to start with towels is because new pups sometimes have accidents in their crates the first few weeks after coming home, and it's much easier to wash towels than big dog beds.

Always use a collar for a puppy and not a harness. While leash training, you will not be able to do corrections with a harness. It will send mixed signals if you try and use both, and consistency is the most important thing when it comes to training. So leave the harness at the store until after the puppy is 1-2 years old.

Also, 6-foot leashes are recommended over 4-foot leashes when training. It gives you the right amount of leash spaced between both of your hands and the dog. Never use retractable leashes in the early years. It causes the dog too much confusion on what's expected of them when out on a leash.

Are there any final thoughts that you feel the readers of this book would benefit from?

Bringing a canine companion into your home can bring more joy than one can ever expect. That joy is only possible if you're ready for the commitment of sharing your life with your new furry friend. They depend on you for everything. They will love you and be loyal to you for the rest of their lives, so be kind to them by knowing if your lifestyle will lend itself to the commitment of sharing your home and time with them before you make the big leap into an adoption.

Thanks so much Malinda for sharing your expertise and just for sharing your unique story with everyone.

Malinda DeVincenzi of Darby Park Doodles
http://www.darbyparkdoodles.com

Glossary

Abdomen – The surface area of a dog's body lying between the chest and the hindquarters; also referred to as the belly.

Allergy – An abnormally sensitive reaction to substances including pollens, foods or microorganisms. May be present in humans or animals with similar symptoms including, but not limited to, sneezing, itching and skin rashes.

Anal Glands – Glands located on either side of a dog's anus used to mark territory. May become blocked and require treatment by a veterinarian.

Arm – On a dog, the region between the shoulder and the elbow is referred to as the arm or the upper arm.

Artificial Insemination – The process by which semen is artificially introduced into the reproductive tract of a female dog for the purposes of a planned pregnancy.

Back – That portion of a dog's body that extends from the withers (or shoulder) to the croup (approximately the area where the back flows into the tail).

Backyard Breeder – Any person engaged in the casual breeding of purebred dogs with no regard to genetic quality or consideration of the breed standard is referred to as a backyard breeder.

Bat Ear – A dog's ear that stands upright from a broad base with a rounded top and a forward-facing opening.

Bitch – The appropriate term for a female dog.

Blooded – An accepted reference to a pedigreed dog.

Breed – A line or race of dogs selected and cultivated by man from a common gene pool to achieve and maintain a characteristic appearance and function.

Breed Standard – A written "picture" of a perfect specimen of a given breed in terms of appearance, movement and behavior as formulated by a parent organization, for example, the American Kennel Club or in Great Britain, The Kennel Club.

Brindle – A marking pattern typically described in conjunction with another color to achieve a layering of black hairs with a lighter color (fawn, brown, or gray) to produce a tiger-striped pattern.

Brows – The contours of the frontal bone that form ridges above a dog's eyes.

Buttocks – The hips or rump of a dog.

Castrate – The process of removing a male dog's testicles.

Chest – That portion of a dog's trunk or body encased by the ribs.

Coat – The hair covering a dog. Most breeds have both an outer coat and an undercoat.

Come Into Season – The point at which a female dog becomes fertile for purposes of mating.

Congenital – Any quality, particularly an abnormality, present at birth.

Crate – Any portable container used to house a dog for transport or provided to a dog in the home as a "den."

Crossbred – Dogs are said to be crossbred when each of their parents is of a different breed.

Dam – A term for the female parent.

Dew Claw – The dew claw is an extra claw on the inside of the leg. It is a rudimentary fifth toe.

Euthanize – The act of relieving the suffering of a terminally ill animal by inducing a humane death, typically with an overdose of anesthesia.

Fancier – Any person with an exceptional interest in purebred dogs and the shows where they are exhibited.

Free Feeding – The practice of making a constant supply of food available for a dog's consumption. Not recommended with Cockapoos.

Groom – To make a dog's coat neat by brushing, combing or trimming.

Harness – A cloth or leather strap shaped to fit the shoulders and chest of a dog with a ring at the top for attaching a lead. An alternative to using a collar.

Haunch Bones – Terminology for the hip bones of a dog.

Haw – The membrane inside the corner of a dog's eye known as the third eyelid.

Head – The cranium and muzzle of a dog.

Hip Dysplasia – A condition in dogs due to a malformation of the hip resulting in painful and limited movement of varying degrees.

Hindquarters – The back portion of a dog's body including the pelvis, thighs, hocks and paws.

Hock – Bones on the hind leg of a dog that form the joint between the second thigh and the metatarsus. Known as the dog's true heel.

Inbreeding – When two dogs of the same breed that are closely related mate.

Kennel – A facility where dogs are housed for breeding or an enclosure where dogs are kept.

Lead – Any strap, cord or chain used to restrain or lead a dog. Typically attached to a collar or harness. Also called a leash.

Litter – The puppy or puppies from a single birth or "whelping."

Muzzle – That portion of a dog's head lying in front of the eyes and consisting of the nasal bone, nostrils and jaws.

Neuter – To castrate or spay a dog thus rendering them incapable of reproducing.

Pedigree –The written record of a pedigreed dog's genealogy. Should extend to three or more generations.

Puppy – Any dog of less than 12 months of age.

Puppy Mill – An establishment that exists for the purpose of breeding as many puppies for sale as possible with no consideration of potential genetic defects.

Rose Ear – Small ears that fold over and back revealing the burr.

Separation Anxiety – The anxiety and stressed suffered by a dog left alone for any period of time.

Sire – The accepted term for the male parent.

Spay – The surgery to remove a female dog's ovaries to prevent conception.

Whelping – Term for the act of giving birth puppies.

Withers – The highest point of a dog's shoulders.

Wrinkle – Any folding and loose skin on the forehead and foreface of a dog.

Photo Credit: Justine Watts of Just Dogz

Index